Member Machine

BUILD YOUR MEMBERSHIP WEBSITE IN JUST 30 DAYS

Callie Willows

Mike Morrison

"The Membership Guys"

Member Machine

First published in 2016 by We Do Digital Ltd t/a The Membership Guys, Great Park, Newcastle upon Tyne, England

This edition first published in 2016 by The Membership Guys
hello@themembershipguys.com

www.themembershipguys.com

ISBN: 978-1-326-87700-2

Contents

Introduction

You don't brand yourselves as "The Membership Guys" if you're not seriously passionate about the membership website model.

So you may consider it biased when we say we believe it to be the absolute best approach to running your business online.

However believe us when we also say that running a membership website has genuinely changed our lives; and the lives of the thousands of people we've helped to create and grow successful memberships of their own.

Escaping the "time for money trap" and saying goodbye to crazy clients with demanding deadlines means we now have a business that not only serves more people and makes more of a difference to our audience; but also brings us far less stress and pressure for far greater reward than running our digital marketing agency ever did.

However, we'd be remiss if we didn't caution you that running a membership website is not for everyone.

If you truly love rolling up your sleeves and working with clients on a one-to-one basis; then the move to the one-to-many model of a membership website may leave you unfulfilled.

If you can't imagine anything worse than creating content, managing a community and handling customer service enquiries then you're not going to like the day to day realities of running a membership.

And of course if you're chasing a silver bullet or golden goose; trying to unlock the secrets of untold riches that pour into your bank account as you kick back on a beach sipping Mai Tais then you're barking up the wrong tree.

However if you relish the opportunity to better leverage your time; to put your skills, knowledge, experience and expertise to greater use; to make a positive difference on a larger scale and to build a stable, reliable stream of ever-accumulating recurring revenue as you do so - then good news. You're reading the right book.

This 30 day guide to launching your own membership gives you the path to follow that will give you the best start for your website.

Each day focuses on a specific area and, most importantly, gives you the action steps you need to take in order to move forward.

You'll also find that we have worksheets included within the book itself. If you'd prefer not to graffiti this magnificent tome, then you can download a bundle containing printable versions and other useful resources at www.membermachine.biz/resources

You will also note that we list various software, plugins and products throughout this book. For brevity we don't include the web address for these with every mention - instead, we've added a resources section at the end of the book with links for anything we mention.

Lastly, while we have structured this as a 30 day process, we understand that for some people this timeframe is simply not achievable for various reasons. If that's you, then consider each day a 'step' that you can follow to a more convenient schedule instead.

We both wish you all the best in planning and building your membership website, and look forward to hearing all about your successful launch!

Callie & Mike

About The Membership Guys

With a combined 25+ years in the online marketing and web development industry, we've been privileged to be involved with hundreds of membership sites, communities and online courses covering a diverse range of topics

From weight loss to business coaching, executive training to bass guitar, and everything in between - we spent years helping great clients to achieve fantastic results from their online business.

Now our focus is on teaching entrepreneurs and small business owners just like you to create successful membership sites which earn 5 - 7 figures a year in recurring revenue.

About Callie Willows

When ill health forced me to reconsider my business, investigating alternative ways to leverage my knowledge and continue helping people led me into the world of digital products and memberships.

I was hooked.

I quickly realised I loved the behind the scenes side of online business more than the subject I was teaching; and I became a little obsessed with figuring out the tech side of memberships and the marketing strategy required to make them a success.

Partnering with Mike was a no-brainer; and after spending years growing successful memberships for our clients I now love nothing more than teaching thousands through our content and our own membership - the Member Site Academy.

About Mike Morrison

I made my first dollar online 17 years ago, and that was enough to hook me on not only figuring out how the tech gubbins of websites worked, but also how to marry that with marketing strategy to build an actual online business.

I've enjoyed a lengthy career, running my own agency and working with businesses of all shapes and sizes - including national brands such as McDonalds, ITV and Ancestry.com - as well as being at the forefront of growing a number of highly successful memberships.

As the host of our podcast (creatively titled "The Membership Guys Podcast") I'm a little fond of the sound of my own voice and I'm partial to the occasional opinionated rant, borne from a passion to help others navigate the murky waters of online marketing.

Connect With Us

Read our blog: www.themembershipguys.com
Listen to the podcast: www.membershippodcast.com
Join our free Facebook group: www.talkmemberships.com
Follow us on Twitter: @membershipguys

And of course if you're REALLY serious about building a successful membership website then you should just the Member Site Academy. The training, resources and community make it an absolute no-brainer for anyone involved with memberships.
Check it out at www.membersiteacademy.com

Deciding on Your Idea

Unsurprisingly, the very first thing you need to create a membership site is an idea. But not just any idea, you need an idea that people are going to want to pay you for. You've probably already got something in mind, but if not, start by brainstorming all the possible subjects you could cover:

- What topics interest you?
- What areas are you most knowledgeable about?
- What problems do you know how to solve?
- Which subjects are people keen to learn about?
- Which topics are people willing to pay to learn about?
- What questions come up frequently in Facebook groups?
- What does your existing audience want to learn about?
- What questions are people asking on social media that relate to your industry?

Once you've brainstormed some ideas narrow it down by asking yourself the following for each idea (and if you already know what your final idea is, run it past these questions too to check for any weak areas):

1. How strong an audience is there for this subject?
2. How much competition exists?
3. How much expertise do you have on this subject?
4. How likely are people to pay to learn about this?
5. How easily can you create content related to this subject?

By doing this you should be able to create a shortlist of 2-3 possible ideas to choose between. Try and keep your ideas as targeted as possible – think niche not broad.

Instead of: *'I'm going to create a membership site about Facebook ads'*

I'm going to teach newbies to become kick-ass VA's!

Try: *'I'm going to teach fitness professionals how to use Facebook ads'.*

The more focused you are with your idea the easier it will be to attract your target audience – ideally you want to be filling a particular gap or solving a specific problem for them.

If you can't decide between ideas, see if there is any way you can merge or combine them. Don't forget to trust your gut instinct as well!

However you decide to do it, pick just one idea to go forward with (you can always keep the others on the backburner for future projects!).

Now for the important bit: The fundamental mistake many people make when creating a membership site is to not validate their idea, or to trust poor methods of validation.

Your family members or your best friend telling you they think your idea is great isn't enough – you need to know that your actual target market want what you're creating.

There are a variety of ways you can validate your idea, from a quick and simple audience survey to creating a full blown 'mini-product'.

Tips for validating your idea

Don't rely on the opinions of your friends and family

I've lost count how many people have approached me with absolutely terrible ideas that they've been convinced are utter genius by their friends and family. While it's completely understandable why most people run their ideas past their loved ones first, very rarely are they the right people to get feedback from.

First and foremost, they care about you, so even the bluntest of best friends and significant others will temper their feedback so as to not offend you if they actually think your idea is rubbish. There's also a chance that if they don't actually understand your idea or concept that they may try to hide this to avoid appearing dumb.

Usually your friends and family won't be the best indicator of your target audience, nor will they have any real understanding or appreciation of the market you're going to be targeting, what works and doesn't work, and what's already out there.

I'm not telling you not to run things past your family and friends at all, just to maintain perspective on the credibility of their input in terms of helping you to validate your idea.

Far too often people go down the wrong route filled with confidence from having everyone close to them tell them how amazing their idea is in an effort to be supportive and positive.

Look at what's already out there

There's no better way to prove that you have a valid and viable idea than if someone is already doing something similar within the same market. Now this is something which does put some people off as they immediately see pre-existing competition as a reason to avoid entering a market, but instead you should see it as a good sign that your idea is one worth pursuing.

The flip-side of this, of course, is coming up with a concept for which there's literally no competition. There's a far greater chance that this means the market and the demand simply do not exist, as opposed to you being the first person in existence to come up with your idea. That's not to say the latter is impossible, just improbable, and so a great deal of further research and idea validation would be needed to really establish whether you're onto a winner or chasing a lost cause.

Look to existing online courses, books, blogs, podcasts and the like for any patterns relating to the subjects being discussed, the level of community engagement and so on; look for what others are doing well, and more importantly what they're doing poorly.

Read through blog comments and book reviews for constructive criticism, particularly as it relates to subjects that people feel aren't being covered, or could be covered better.

Get a good idea of what's going on within the market, what is and isn't working and where the opportunities lie, and this will give you a good basis for validating your own idea and adapting it so that you can come in with a fresh approach on a topic that there's clearly an established market for.

Start Collecting Leads Early

The main thing we're looking to validate is that there are people out there who will be interested in what you have to say and what knowledge you have to impart on a particular subject.

The actual specifics aren't important yet – it doesn't matter at this stage whether you're thinking of a full blown membership site, ebook or video course; if your basic idea sucks, the "delivery method" won't make a difference.

So what better way of validating that people are interested than actually capturing their interest – specifically their email address, submitted as an indication that they want more information.

Using a service such as Leadpages or Unbounce you can get a basic landing page set up within minutes, and then hook it up to an email marketing service such as Aweber in order to start collecting email addresses.

You can choose whether to "bribe" interested parties with a free giveaway (such as an ebook, infographic or short video), or you could go with a "coming soon" approach whereby you give a rough outline of the sort of thing you'll eventually be offering and allow people to "register their interest" by submitting their email address in order to be sent future updates.

Then it's simply a case of pushing traffic to your landing page – either organically by promoting it on social media or to an existing email list – or by using pay-per-click (PPC) advertising.

Assuming your call to action and the landing page itself are half decent you should be able to get an initial read on whether there's any interest in your idea or not.

Test the market with a 'minimum viable product'

One step up on simply collecting leads to establish that there's a potential market out there interested in what you're going to offer is to actually try to get people to buy something that's in the same ballpark, by offering them a minimum viable product.

A "minimum viable product" – or "MVP" to use the ever-so trendy lingo – is an offering in the same vein as your intended final product, targeting the same audience, but done in such a way that doesn't require as much upfront work, time and financial investment to get going.

Note that this doesn't mean a "rushed" version of your final product – more something that will achieve the same objectives for your customer as you hope to achieve with your final product, but in a manner that doesn't require too much input to "go to market".

So, for example:

If you're planning on developing a course teaching people how to play the trumpet, you could test the viability of this by offering a set amount of 1-2-1 Skype lessons

If you want to build a paid coaching community online, then you could do a trial run with an MVP consisting of a series of group coaching calls supplemented by a private Facebook group.

Or if your idea is to create a series of lessons teaching someone how to use a particular piece of software, you could first try an MVP of a brief ebook that focuses on one specific area of that software.

These are just some basic examples, but hopefully you'll see the pattern emerging – your MVP would be something that requires very little effort to get it to a stage where you can try to get some customers, rather than spending hours creating a product only to find out nobody wants to buy.

Testing the market with a minimum viable product is a great way to establish that the demand for what you're offering exists, and to save you a lot of time, effort and disappointment in the long run.

Day One: Action Steps

1. Using the questions from this chapter, finalise your idea for your membership site.

2. Decide on a method of validation that you will use to check that your idea has potential.

Fleshing Out Your Idea

Yesterday we looked at your idea for your membership site and today we're going to take that idea and flesh it out even further.

Spend some time thinking about the following questions:

1. **What information/resources can you provide** on your topic?
2. **What is the goal of your site** – what will members achieve?
3. **Does the topic provide enough content** for an ongoing membership site, or is it more suitable to a course?
4. **Who are your audience** and where will you reach them?
5. **What are the competition doing** and what will you do differently? *(Remember: don't just look at other membership sites, what else is out there that relates to your idea?)*
6. **How will you provide value** to your members?
7. **What would be your ideal membership site?** *(Don't worry about technical details right now)*
8. **What does success "look like" for you** in terms of your membership site? *(i.e. number of members, revenue etc)*

Putting some meat on the bones like this is an important step so don't rush yourself if any of your answers aren't clear or you need to do further research.

Day Two: Action Steps

1. Complete the activity above – the more details the better.

2. Complete our idea worksheet on the next page. This will act as cliff notes to focus on the most important aspects of your idea whilst you work through the rest of the challenge.

Your Idea Worksheet

Complete the following questions to finalise your ideas for your membership site.

What will your membership site be about?

What will be the main subject of your site? Can this be broken down into sections?

How to establish yourself as a VA. Broken up
into stages of setting up a business, provide
tools, templates + advice

Why have you chosen this subject?

Is it something you're especially passionate about? Something you have a lot of knowledge about?

I struggled to get set-up, there are some
things that I've still not done. It would
have been good to have one place with
direct access to 'people in the know'

Who is your target market or ideal member for the site?

The more specific you can be the better!

Someone who isn't too familiar with what is needed to become a VA, what processes they need to follow, what is needed out there but has some skills required to be a VA.

What will members learn? What problem are you solving?

Why would someone join your site – what's in it for them? What need are you fixing?

What solution are you offering?

A full start to end journey of setting up as a VA providing tools + resources to establish themselves. Removing the nerves + uncertainty that so many have.

How will your idea be different to other solutions out there?

What are your competitors offering and how will you distinguish yourself from them?

It's one place where everything is for all resources/tools. It's a private area for people in the situation to get together + develop/learn.

What are your initial goals for the site?

What does success look like to you? E.g. 50 members at launch, $2000 a month income, happy testimonials from members?

Happy testimonials from members. Being able to see the positive impact the site is having on people. I just like to help!

Additional Notes

Any other thoughts and ideas you have at this stage:

Maybe need to consider recurring revenue. How keep VA's on the site even when they are established. Don't just want people to leave.

What audience - consider differences between other places than UK.

This could be a strong forum opportunity - people just need the reassurance!

Two stage site - set-up new VA's then offer different rate to keep them in a community?

Creating Your Launch Plan

You may be wondering why we've gone straight from idea to launch, but have no fear, we're right on track and you haven't missed anything!

The truth is that the most important factor in a successful membership site (other than great content!) is an audience. Or, to put it bluntly, someone to buy it.

You could bust a gut creating a wonderful membership site, but if no one sees it, it's all been for nothing (and we hate to break it to you but build it and they will come is a total myth!)

So, with that in mind, before we get into the nitty gritty of your membership site we want to make sure that you have a launch plan in place and that, whilst you're busy building your site, you're also generating a list of people who might want to join once it's completed.

Let's take a look at your existing audience first (if you have one):

- Do you have a good following on Facebook or Twitter (or whatever your chosen social media platforms are)?
- Do you have an existing email list?
- Does your current website or blog receive much traffic?
- Most importantly, is this existing audience the same audience that your membership site will be aimed at?

If the answer to the above questions is yes then great! But don't worry if you don't already have a large audience. Whilst it might make life easier, it's better to have 100 highly engaged subscribers than 10000 who don't really care about you and what you're offering.

Tomorrow we're going to be looking at how to start building a waiting list for your site, but that's only a small part of your launch plan. You also want to think about the kind of launch content that you will need to create, who else you can get involved in the launch to help spread the word, whether or not you want to do interviews, webinars and guest posts or simply drive traffic to your own blog, not to mention what kind of launch strategy you will follow...and so on!

The more time you give yourself and the earlier you put a plan in place, the better prepared you will be to come flying out of the gates when you launch your site.

Launch Strategies

A good membership site launch plan needs to:

- Increase awareness
- Raise interest
- Build demand

By doing this you put yourself in the best possible position to succeed when you open the doors.

The following 5 strategies are straightforward but effective, and can easily be combined with your existing launch plans to make sure your membership site gets off to a good start:

Offer a free video training course

Perhaps the most well known strategy for launching an information product, membership site or online course is Jeff Walker's Product

Launch Formula.

While the strategy itself has various elements to it, it essentially boils down to:

- Offer a free 3 part course on a topic related to your product as a "lead magnet"
- Deliver the course one video at a time, over 1-2 weeks
- Ensure that not only does each video teach something, but that they also highlight the need for your product
- End the course with a lead-in to your upcoming product launch

There's a great deal more psychology and nuance to what Walker teaches, and if you'd like to dig further then I'd recommend checking out his book "Launch" which covers this strategy in depth.

Run a launch webinar

Webinars are extremely popular these days, and for good reason.

Assuming your membership site revolves around educational content, then it makes sense that a good place to start for finding new members is to tap into people who demonstrate a desire to learn something about your topic.

Offering a live webinar on a relevant topic is a great way to generate qualified leads, teach them something of value and then introduce them to your product.

The live aspect is particularly instrumental in supporting any 'scarcity tactics' you employ in your pitch, such as a limited window for discounted pricing.

Run a teaser campaign to your existing audience.

As soon as you have a pretty good idea of what it is that you're going to be offering, it's a good idea to put some form of "waiting list" online so that you can start gathering leads early.

Once those people have joined your waiting list, it's a good idea to check in with them from time to time in order to update them on progress and whet their appetites for your forthcoming membership site.

As you move closer to the actual launch of your site then you can start this up; periodically sending information to your audience as well as posting "teasers" across your social media channel with tidbits of information about what's coming up.

Your teasers could include:

- Details on when you're launching, with a periodic "countdown" along the lines of "Only 4 weeks to go until…"
- Information about what your product will actually consist of, teased in the form of "Today we're wrapping things up on our course about widgets and doohickeys – I think members are going to love this when we open in a few weeks"
- Screenshots of your dashboard, course pages etc, or even behind the scenes videos

Orchestrate a content blitz

Notice that whenever a movie comes out, its stars seem to pop up in every magazine interview, entertainment blog and TV chat show?

They become ambassadors for the forthcoming release, tasked with raising awareness and getting people excited and interested in seeing it.

You need to become that for your upcoming product launch.

Strategically seeking out the blogs and podcasts that are popular with your market and arranging guest blogging and interview opportunities is an extremely effective way of leveraging other people's audience to publicise and promote your membership site.

All of this should, of course, be complemented by ramping up your own content marketing efforts with a broad mix of material that all leads in to your membership site or online course.

Offer special launch pricing and bonuses

Scarcity is proven to be a very powerful factor in generating sales.

Launches present us with a fantastic opportunity for leveraging genuine scarcity (our favourite kind!), so it's very much worth tapping into that for the release of your own membership site or online course.

If you're going to be running a time-sensitive product then this scarcity will be baked in since you'll have specific opening and close dates or limits on the number of enrolments; so you should be emphasising this as much as possible.

For evergreen products the simplest way to leverage scarcity is to offer discounted, introductory pricing during your launch period.

We recommend limiting the discount to a specific time period rather than limiting it to, say, the first 100 members; as if you do the latter and two weeks later the offer is still available it will be clear you're still not at 100 members, which doesn't reflect well on you!

Same goes for launch bonuses too – you can offer additional training, bonus add-on products, exclusive one-on-one sessions with you, or anything else you may think of to add value for early adopters.

Want more ideas? Observe how other people run their own product launches

Reverse engineering the marketing activities of other businesses is a great way of getting insight and ideas for your own project, so keep an eye out for anyone with a launch coming up and pay attention to what they do.

Day Three: Action Steps

1. Complete the launch worksheet on the next page.

2. Create a launch calendar with the dates of when you plan to launch and when you plan to release specific pieces of pre-launch and launch content. If you plan on doing things like guest interviews and blog posts then get these booked up with the relevant people in advance.

Your Launch Worksheet

Complete the following questions to develop your launch plan

Decide on your launch timeframe

How long do you need to create everything? What date do you want the site to go live?

How long will your launch last for? Will you be closing the site after your launch period?

What pre-launch marketing can you do?

Use the time before your launch to start building hype and interest in your membership site. Tick the options below that you could use:

- ☐ Email your list letting them know something exciting is coming.
- ☐ Share sneak-peeks of what you're creating via your social media accounts and blog.
- ☐ Write blog posts that showcase your expertise, provide value and relate to your upcoming membership site.
- ☐ Add a coming soon or launch image to your website sidebar.
- ☐ Post across social media about your upcoming launch.
- ☐ Let any communities (online and offline) know what you're working on.
- ☐ Include a P.S. mentioning your upcoming product in your emails.

Any other pre-launch ideas?

Think about your connections, specific resources at your disposal that others may not have access to.

How will you promote your launch?

The doors are open! Tick the options below that you could use to get the word out about your new membership site once you launch:

- ☐ Send an email sequence to your list – several emails throughout the launch.
- ☐ Write valuable blog content with a clear call to action for your membership.
- ☐ Create a free video sequence that leads into your membership.
- ☐ Run a live webinar on a related topic.
- ☐ Set up an affiliate program for your supporters.
- ☐ Line up some interviews and guest posts to get in front of a larger audience.
- ☐ Make use of paid traffic such as Facebook Ads (but don't forget that Twitter, YouTube, Pinterest or Google ads may be more suitable for your audience)
- ☐ Run remarketing campaigns to target website visitors
- ☐ Run a contest for a free membership or other relevant prize.
- ☐ Create shareable graphics for social media and your website.
- ☐ Run a live Q&A session to answer any questions.

- ☐ Create a sneak peak video of inside your membership site.
- ☐ Run a 7 day trial so that people can see how great your site is.
- ☐ Run a 5-30 day email challenge.
- ☐ Create an early-bird pricing option.
- ☐ Develop some special bonuses for members who join during the launch period.

Any other ideas for your launch period?

```



```

Based on the above answers what launch content do you need to create?

Will you need to create blog posts, podcasts, webinars, new opt-in freebies?

```



```

Who can be your launch support?

Who can you ask to help you promote the launch, perhaps by doing guest interviews or blog posts?

What are your launch goals?

How many members would you like to gain over your launch period? How many email signups? How much revenue would you like to make?

Building a Wait-List Page

As we mentioned yesterday, it's important to start building an audience for your membership site as early as possible rather than waiting until you're actually ready to launch your site.

So, whatever your current audience size, one of the first things you should do once you know you're setting up a membership site or online course is to create a landing page and start building an email list of interested parties.

You may want to use your existing website for this (if you have one), an external service like LeadPages, or you may want to install WordPress on a domain just for your new membership site (this is our preferred method).

There are a number of different ways to create a landing page.

Common options include:

- **LeadPages** *(www.leadpages.net)* is a third-party software so can be used on its own, but it can also be integrated with your WordPress site if you have one. It has a number of tried and tested templates that are easy to set up – but they are lacking in customisability. There is a monthly or yearly fee for use.
- **ClickFunnels** *(www.clickfunnels.com)* is a third-party system designed for creating complete sales and marketing funnels. It makes use of page templates, however these are more customisable than the LeadPages options. Payment is monthly.
- **OptimizePress** *(www.optimizepress.com)* is a theme and plugin for WordPress which can be installed on either your existing website or a new one. It has a number of inbuilt templates that you can customise completely, or you can create your own

design from scratch. Your license is valid for a minimum of 3 sites, and renewable yearly to receive updates.

- **Thrive Content Builder** *(www.thrivethemes.com)* is a plugin that can be used with any WordPress site. It has landing page templates inbuilt but is also a visual editor that makes it easy to create any design you can think of – and it can be used on normal WordPress pages and posts as well as creating landing pages. Again there's a yearly fee for renewals.
- **Coming Soon Plugins** are also an option if you want to save money and don't need anything fancy. If you search the plugin repository you'll find quite a few options – **Coming Soon Pro** by SeedProd *(www.seedprod.com)* is a solid choice.

Our personal favourite, having used the alternatives, is Thrive Content Builder.

We've recorded a video to show you how to quickly and easily set up your landing page with Thrive which is available free at *www.tmgys. co/thrivewalkthrough*

What to include on your landing page

- **A synopsis of what you are creating** – this doesn't need to give all the details or go in-depth, but should give some idea of what people are signing up for and if possible an idea of when it will be available. You could use a video as well if you wanted to.
- **An opt-in form** – this goes without saying but you need this to collect the names and emails of interested people. This will be hooked up to your email marketing service and you can then send emails to your wait list in the build up to your launch.
- **A free gift** – it's great to generate interest and showcase your

expertise by giving away something of value. This could be a short e-book on a topic related to your membership site, it could be access to a Facebook group, or even just a simple one page checklist or top tools list.

A free gift isn't essential for a wait list, but it will often increase the number of sign-ups and can be a good way of getting people to want more of your content.

As you may have noticed, creating a landing page and wait list is also one of the methods of validation mentioned way back on day 1, so as you're building your list, you're also proving that there is a need for your product.

Day Four: Action Steps

1. **Choose a landing page tool** and set up your waitlist page – this doesn't need to have lots of bells and whistles.

2. **Start promoting this page** to your existing audience if you have one.

3. **Plan ways to drive new traffic to your landing page** – you could do this via blog posts, social media or even paid tools like Facebook ads (refer back to your launch sheet from Day 3).

Figuring Out Your Features

So far, we've got our idea, we know when we plan to launch and we're already building up our wait list. Now we're going to start getting into the nitty gritty of your actual membership site.

Over the next few days we're going to be looking at your membership model, your site structure and, today, the membership features you want your site to have. All of which will help us greatly when we come to choose our membership plugin and actually build our site.

When we talk about features we are, for the most part, actually talking about functionality, which can typically be broken down into two different types:

- **Backend** – the functionality you need for the smooth running of your site
- **Frontend** – the functionality that enhances the site for your members

Knowing what features you need and want from your site is essential in helping you to choose the right membership plugin, so it's important to think about everything you might need.

The last thing you want to do is choose and set up a plugin, only to decide that you want an additional feature that it doesn't include or integrate with (trust us, this is never fun!).

Back on day 2 we asked you to think about your ideal membership site, and you may like to refer back to those notes when you think about your feature needs.

Some features might seem obvious, but you'd be surprised how easy it is to forget something (or to have not considered it at all) and something you consider an obvious feature might not be needed by somebody else.

Some things to consider:

- Some features will not be part of your membership plugin itself, and therefore will rely on getting different technologies to work together (i.e. delivering live training/webinars).
- Don't worry if you don't actually need many features – simple doesn't equal bad.
- Similarly, don't fall into the trap of wanting everything. Think about what will actually be beneficial to your members.
- Think about your future needs as well, for example you may not want an affiliate system to begin with, but will you want one in a few months?

Day Five: Action Steps

1. Complete our **Features Checklist** on the next page.

2. If you're not 100% sure on what features you want, **spend some time researching what other membership sites are offering and what you do and don't like.**

Your Membership Features

Select from the list below the features that you need for your membership. We recommend using 2 different colours when checking off your choices; one for features that are essential and the other for features that are a 'like to have'.

- ☐ Protected pages
- ☐ Dripped (time released) content
- ☐ On-Site Forum
- ☐ Private Facebook group
- ☐ Other community (Slack, Google+)
- ☐ Affiliate System
- ☐ Course structure (modules/ lessons)
- ☐ Quizzes or assessments
- ☐ Live webinars/hangouts
- ☐ Live calls
- ☐ Interviews
- ☐ Comments on content
- ☐ Protected PDF downloads
- ☐ Audio streaming
- ☐ Audio downloads
- ☐ Video streaming
- ☐ Free or paid trials
- ☐ Member profiles
- ☐ Member directory
- ☐ Private messaging system
- ☐ Member feedback/reviews
- ☐ Gamification (e.g. badges/ leaderboard)
- ☐ Additional non-membership products
- ☐ Credit or token system
- ☐ Coupons or discount codes
- ☐ Secure RSS feeds
- ☐ Recurring payments
- ☐ Non-recurring payments
- ☐ Instalment payments
- ☐ Sneak peeks of protected content
- ☐ Partial content protection
- ☐ Paywall capabilities
- ☐ Video downloads
- ☐ Other file types
- ☐ Upsells
- ☐ Downsells
- ☐ One-time offers
- ☐ Upgrade paths/tiered memberships
- ☐ Consecutive memberships

- ☐ Multiple membership levels
- ☐ Group/company memberships
- ☐ Start dates for content delivery
- ☐ Automated cancellations
- ☐ Ability to pause membership
- ☐ Pro-rated membership upgrades
- ☐ Ability for members to upload files
- ☐ Surveys or forms
- ☐ Member reports e.g sales, retention
- ☐ Social logins
- ☐ Tax/VAT capabilities

Do you need any other features not mentioned here?

Choosing Your Membership Model

Your membership model is the backbone of your site and dictates the type of membership that you are actual running.

While you'll find lots of variations of membership models, we actually split this into 3 separate types of models that you can combine as you need.

The 3 different models that make up your overall membership model:

- **Content** – the main type of content you will be offering
- **Delivery** – the way your content will be delivered
- **Access** – how long members can access your content for

Essentially you need to pick one option from each of these models, and combined they will create your membership model. This gives you quite a lot of flexibility, rather than tying you to a model that isn't quite the right fit.

The Content Model

Content models can be broken down into 6 different types:

- **Course** – a structured course with an a-z path, broken into modules/lessons (or similar) and with a particular goal.
- **Premium content** – providing in-depth content that's either standalone or structured differently from a course.
- **Library** – a content hub comprising of lots of different courses or content types, usually with a 'pic'n'mix' approach.
- **Community** – a forum or other group brought together to discuss a particular topic.
- **Service** – accompanies a service such as coaching, design or web fixes (e.g monthly design graphics).

- **Product** – a digital product or resource – usually downloadable.

Your content model should be based on the main focus of your site. So, you may plan on having a community element, but if your main offering is a 6 month course, your content model is the course.

The Delivery Model

How will you deliver you content to members? There's just 3 options to choose from here:

- **Instant** – everything is available immediately. No new content to be added except perhaps updates or bonuses.
- **Ongoing** – new content released on an ongoing basis – usually monthly and often without an end date.
- **Dripped** – content released at scheduled intervals relative to when the member joins. Often for a set amount of time.

The Access Model

Your access model is linked to the payment structure you will have, as payment dictates whether someone has access.

There are 4 main options to choose from here.

- **Recurring** – access tied to regular payments, usually monthly. When payment stops access is removed.
- **Lifetime** – access for as long as the content is available.
- **Fixed Term** – access for a set amount of time, i.e. 12 months.
- **Pay As You Go** – access as needed.

Lifetime and fixed term options could be either one-off or instalment payments (or both). If using instalments, then be aware that the access can still be revoked if someone fails to make one of their payments.

The Pay As You Go Model is lesser known but think of sites like Udemy or Skillshare – you become a member and then pay for access to specific courses as you need them. This model is also common in the fitness world for access to workout videos.

You may offer a combination of payment methods, such as recurring and lifetime, but your access model will depend on the predominant one – usually the recurring option if this is offered.

Day Six: Action Steps

1. Complete the Membership Model Sheet on the next page and decide on the content, delivery and access model for your site. If there are any variables to your model make sure you make a note of this too.

Your Membership Model

Complete the following questions to confirm your content, access and delivery models.

What will be the content model for your membership site?

☐ Course   ☐ Community

☐ Premium   ☐ Service

☐ Library   ☐ Product

What will be the delivery model for your membership site?

☐ Instant   ☐ Ongoing   ☐ Dripped

Ongoing delivery: with what frequency will you release content?

Dripped: how often will content be released and over what period?

What will be the access model for your membership site?

☐ Recurring

What frequency (e.g. monthly) and how long for:

☐ Lifetime

One-off payment, instalments or both:

☐ Fixed Term

How long for? One-off payment, instalments or both:

☐ Pay As You Go

Will there also be a joining fee:

Your Website Structure

So, we know our feature set and we know our membership model, but now we need to create our site structure so that everything has its place on our site.

When we talk about structure we're mainly talking about what pages you want to have, how they will all fit together and also how your members will navigate around your site and find everything that they need.

Some things to consider:

- **What system pages do you need?** These are the functional pages like your account page, member dashboard or welcome page, profile page, cancellation page, login page etc.
- **How many different types of content pages do you require?** Do you need different page layouts for video content and text content?
- **What pages do you need for additional functionality?** Think about pages for affiliate content, forum pages, a member directory (you may want to refer back to your features list).
- **Don't forget your sales page and any landing pages or launch pages!**

Next, think about how all your pages will work together. What's the natural and logical flow between them?

A great exercise to is to grab a stack of Post-It notes and on each write down the name of a website page or section. Then, find some space on a wall and position your Post-Its according to how you see your site being structured. Starting with the homepage, then below that your main sections, breaking down further into specific pages.

Below is an example of how you could structure your top level pages:

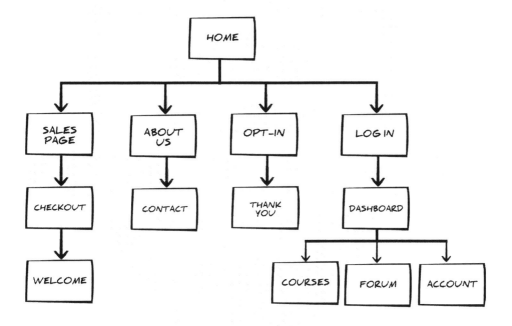

Day Seven: Action Steps

1. **Using the questions above as a prompt, write down all the pages you need for your site.** Be as specific as you can

2. Once you have your list of pages, **create your own sitemap** like the above example. We'll be referring to this as you create your site.

Don't worry if your sitemap isn't perfect, you can add things later, but try to make sure you have all the essential pages that you need and want, even if you're not quite sure of the best way to link them up yet.

DAY 8

The Value of Community

Today we're taking a little side-step to talk about building a community as part of your membership.

Now, when deciding on your membership features the other day you may have already accounted for this aspect, but if you haven't you might want to have a little rethink as your community is often vital in making your site a success.

Why is community so key?

We've talked before on our blog about the value of having a community for increasing member engagement, and it's something we consider all membership sites should have in one way or another.

Including a community in your membership site has a number of benefits, for both you and your members.

Benefits to members:

- **Improves learning** and offers a space to talk more in-depth on the subject, as well as ask questions and share experiences with other members.
- **Creates a sense of connection** and a space for networking and friendships to occur, increasing the value of your membership.
- **Provides a way of obtaining feedback and support**, from both yourself and other members.

Benefits to you:

- **Lightens the load** and takes the pressure off you to answer every question your members have, as they can ask the community instead.

- **Provides an ongoing resource** for you to use to create future content, by giving you the opportunity to see what your members need and want.
- **Improves retention of your membership** – members may join for the content but they stay for the community.

Exceptions to the rule:

While we feel that creating a community is essential to most membership sites success, there are some notable exceptions.

If you're creating a service based or product based membership, or a completely standalone DIY course with no involvement from you, then you can forgo the community.

However, a support forum or Facebook group is still a good idea to provide some after-sale support and respond to any questions.

Different ways of creating a community:

There are a variety of different ways that you can add a community to your membership, some more technical than others.

- **An on-site forum** using a tool like bbPress, Simple:Press, Vanilla Forums, Xenforo or IP.Board.
- **An on-site social network** using a tool like Buddypress
- **A Facebook group, LinkedIn Group or Google+ Group** – meet your audience where they already are.
- **A Slack group** – this tool is quite new but increasing in popularity.
- **Comments** – simply turning WordPress comments on so that members can discuss each pages content individually.

- **Live hangouts or webinars** using a tool like Google Hangouts or uStream.

We recommend using an on-site forum rather than setting up a social media group. The main reason for this is because you have no control over what companies like Facebook may decide to do with your group. If they decide your group breaks their rules, they'll close it down. If they choose to remove the groups feature, you'll have no say.

We've seen countless examples of people using Facebook groups for their paid members where the group has been deleted overnight. We're big fans of free Facebook groups (in fact we run a popular one at www.talkmemberships.com) but when it comes to paying members we always advise to build your community on your own turf.

Day Eight: Action Steps

1. Decide on the type of community you would like for your site. Add this to your Features list if it's not already there.

2. Decide on the software you will use – particularly if you are going the forum or social network route as this may affect your membership plugin choice.

3. Think about how you'll encourage member engagement in your community– what topics can you encourage discussion around, what questions can you ask, could you run challenges or have certain days of the week for specific themes or discussions?

Deciding What to Charge

Have you decided what to charge for your membership site yet?

You may well have thought about it as you completed the last few days of the challenge, however it's something that lots of people struggle with. How do you put a value on your content?

The first thing you should think about is whether you're going to offer recurring or non-recurring payments – or even both. In fact, you've probably already decided this when looking at which Access Model you were going to use on day 6. To recap though:

Recurring payments are the norm for standard membership sites, with payment typically being monthly and in the range of $7 – $97 (but much higher priced options do exist!).

The implementation of recurring payments is a little more involved as you want to ensure that if a payment isn't made then access to your content is revoked – however this is easily done with most membership plugins.

Obviously you are also allowing members the chance to cancel with this option, so when working out your pricing it's useful to also think about how long you think the average member will stay with you.

Non-recurring payments are typically much simpler – people pay, they get access to the content and, short of asking for a refund, that's all there is to it and that money is in the bank.

One-off payments are typically for higher amounts – how high depends on the exact type of membership you're creating and the content provided. If you're releasing new content monthly, a one-off option (yearly or lifetime) is usually, but not always, in addition to a recurring option rather than the only choice, and yearly pricing would typically be the equivalent of 10 monthly payments.

A note about courses: If your membership site is for a single course (or signature programme), pricing options tend to be either one-off or instalments and in general pricing is often higher.

Instalments aren't the same as recurring payments – these are when you split up the one-off price into a set number of payments (typically 2-4) to allow people to spread out the cost. There is still the risk of members cancelling or missing payments with this option though.

So how do you work out your price?

There are a number of ways to work out how to price your product, such as:

- **Looking at what your competitors are charging** and how your product compares.
- **Working out the value** that the end result has for your member.
- **Surveying your audience** and seeing what price range they would be willing to pay.
- **Thinking about where you want to position yourself in the marketplace** – are you hoping to reach as many people as possible or to be an exclusive high end option?
- **Working out how many monthly members you would like and how much you want to earn** monthly and then determining the monthly fee needed to achieve that (e.g. if you want to make $1000 a month and have 50 members you would need to charge $20 a month).

At the end of the day the only "rule" there really is with pricing is that your price should fall in-between the amount it costs you to produce and how much your audience would be willing to pay. If you're an expert in your field, offering 1-2-1 support and a guaranteed result, then your pricing can be a lot higher than for a DIY course with no support.

And remember, it can be easier to put the price up later than to lower it! Although you can obviously introduce discounts if you feel people aren't buying due to price alone.

Think About Offering a Choice

You may also want to consider offering variations of your membership, with a lower level, mid-level and high level price – for example your main content could stay the same but the level of support provided alters for each level.

Offering tiers enables you to appeal to a wider range of budgets without detracting from the value of your actual product. Don't use more than 3 tiers though as too much choice just leads to confusion!

The Value of Trials

You may also like to consider whether you want to offer a trial of your product – either free or for a nominal fee like $1.

Trials can be a great way of reducing the risk members take signing up to your site, similar to a guarantee but with the benefit of allowing members to see 'under the hood' of your site before parting with their hard earned cash.

When considering whether to join your membership site or purchase your online course, your potential customer has a great number of questions going through their mind...

- Is this person or company really as good as they say they are?
- Will this membership be everything they promise it will be?
- Have I really understood what they're offering?
- Is it going to be worth the money?
- What happens if I'm not happy or have made a mistake joining?
- Are they just going to take my money and run?

Now try as you might to address these and the multitude of other concerns a potential member might have through your sales page copy, emails etc; there will almost always still be unanswered questions, so in truth anyone joining your site is taking a little bit of a risk.

That's why top-level marketers such as Jay Abraham espouse the importance of "risk reversal" – incorporating a strategy that seeks to eliminate the risk a user takes when choosing to do business with you.

Often this materialises in the form of money back guarantees, but trial periods are also a great method of risk reversal that enables you to address potential customer concerns that could be getting in the way of your sales.

The most important thing is that a trial gets people into your wheelhouse and gives you an opportunity to prove why your membership site is one that they need to be a part of. By giving people just enough time to get stuck into your product, to become introduced to your business and your community, you stand a better chance of making them want to stick around.

You're also able to create the "fear of disconnect", by showing people what they're missing out on if they don't continue on into full membership of your site beyond their trial period.

When not to offer a trial

Typically if your product is an online course rather than a membership site, a trial likely won't be your best option as it's far more likely that someone could breeze through your course during their trial window. In fact they may see doing so as a challenge.

Often course owners will drip feed their lessons in order to either prolong membership length or to give students more time to engage with the content – again this is an approach for which a trial would be ineffective.

An alternative strategy you could try is having a basic/free level of membership whereby people register an account on your site in order to access a scaled back version of your offering on a permanent basis. This at least gets people into your community and gives you a means of exposing them to your core offering and encouraging them to upgrade their membership.

Day Nine: Action Steps

1. Complete our **pricing worksheet** on the next page to help you figure out your price range.

Your Pricing Worksheet

Answer the following questions to help determine your price point.

How much can your audience afford to pay?

What are they already buying in this space? How affluent are they?

What level of support and contact is provided?

How much access will they have to you? Will contact be on a 1-to-1 or 1-to-many basis?

How valuable will the results be to your members?

Are you offering a tangible result? Is this result personal, financial or business related?

How much are your competitors charging?

How does your offering compare – are you providing more or less?

How well known are you in this market?

Are you perceived as an expert on this subject and do you have a large audience?

Are you offering a course or a membership site?

If you're offering a course how long does it last for, is it evergreen or open/close? If a membership site is it ongoing with continuous new content, or fixed content?

How much do you need to make to break even?

What are your production costs? Will you have ongoing monthly costs? Don't forget to factor in your own time!

How much would you like to make?

What value do you place on your product? What price would you be happy receiving?

Will you be offering different membership tiers?

Are you going to have several different packages available?

What pricing structure will you be using?

☐ Recurring   ☐ Annual

☐ Lifetime   ☐ Instalments

Bearing all the above factors in mind, how will you price your membership site?

Developing Your Brand

Today we're going to take a look at how you're going to brand your membership site.

Now, we're not branding strategists so this isn't an in-depth look at all things brand related, but here are some of the things you need to bear in mind when it comes to your membership:

1. **Where will your membership live** – are you going to be housing your membership on your existing website, a subdomain, or its own shiny new domain? Your choice will impact your branding options as if your membership site is simply an add-on to your existing website, you will most likely want to keep the same colours and styles.

2. **It's not just about the visuals** – your site name, logo and colour scheme aren't your brand. Yes, they are important but in reality they are just 'shorthand' for what people think and feel when they come across your business. So, before you pick out a pretty colour scheme first recognise what impression you are aiming to make.

3. **Consistency is king** – make sure that your website, social media and advertising all line up and give the same message and impression. We're not just talking visual consistency here (although that's important!) but also the tone you use in all your content and communications.

4. **Don't overthink the name** – if you need to spend a paragraph of your sales page explaining what your membership site name means, you've overthought things. Keep it simple, memorable and understandable – clarity wins over clever in this instance. That's not to say that you can't come up with something fun or quirky, just make sure people aren't having to think too hard to work out what your product is.

5. **Make sure your team is on board** – anyone contributing to your site needs to have the same values that you want your brand to represent in order to achieve that key consistency that we mentioned previously. If you hire someone to run your Facebook Ads for you, make sure they understand what you're all about first.

Day Ten: Action Steps

1. Complete our **branding worksheet** on the next page to get a better feel for your membership brand.

Your Branding Worksheet

Think about your membership site brand. What do you want to happen when people hear your name or see your logo?

I want them to feel...

I want them to think...

I want them to remember...

I want them to know...

Write down 5 potential names for your membership

Try tying the name into the content model, topic or end result of your site. For example for a mastermind about increasing sales, consider the Sales Success Mastermind.

1. _____

2. _____

3. _____

4. _____

5. _____

What colour scheme will you use?

Take a look at design-seeds.com for some inspiration. Write down hex codes of your chosen colours below as you'll need them when building your site (find hex codes on Design Seeds by hovering over the colour – you will see a code in a format like #66009

What fonts will you use?

What fonts represent your brand? You want to choose just 2-3 fonts to use throughout your site and graphics. We recommend Google web fonts.

Creating Your Membership Content

Now that we know the kind of membership site we're going to create and how we want it to function and feel, it's time to talk about content.

Your content is really the lifeblood of your membership site. It's what your members are paying for and you want it to deliver everything you've promised – and more if possible.

Creating your membership content is likely to be the most time consuming part of building your membership site, so if you haven't already started doing it, now is the time!

Types of content you could use:

- **Screenshare videos** – typically used for a slide presentation with a voiceover or a tutorial such as a plugin walkthrough.
- **Face-to-camera videos** – useful for connecting with the audience and discussing topics without a need for visuals.
- **Audio recordings** – these may be completely new content, such as interviews, or simply the audio stripped from your videos.
- **Worksheets/PDFs** – these are usually downloadable files for your members, often containing exercises to accompany your other content.
- **Text** – some of your content may just be simple text pages or posts on your site. It's a good idea to include a visual or images as well if possible.
- **Webinars** – this is usually content that is streamed live using something like GoToWebinar or Google Hangouts. Recordings can then be added to the membership too for those who don't make it live.

How you create your content will depend on its format and the tools you have available.

Where possible it's a good idea to offer a variety of different formats to accommodate people's different learning styles – this could be as simple as offering a transcript alongside a video for those who prefer text.

Some content creation considerations:

- **Get the equipment right** – this is especially important for video content. Make sure you have a good mic for sound quality and a decent camera and lighting if doing face-to-camera videos. This doesn't have to be expensive! Check out our friends at emmywu.com or savvysexysocial.com for tips on equipment and how to get your videos right.
- **Don't skimp on editing** – for screenshare videos invest in something like Screenflow or Camtasia to make the recording and editing process easier. For audio files, auphonic.com provides some good, free, post-production options. For text or workbooks, make sure you proof-read thoroughly for typos!
- **What do you need before launch** – you may not actually need to create all your content before you launch your membership. For example, if you're running a 6 month course with content dripped out monthly, you can just make sure you have the first months content created. If you're running a library site however, you're likely going to want to launch with a few different pieces of content ready to go.
- **Have a plan** – it always takes longer than you think to create your content. Make sure you have a plan in place for what you need to create, what will be done when, and how you're going

to do it. And ensure you have a little leeway before your site goes live.

- **Hire out** – consider outsourcing certain elements of your content creation if you can. Perhaps you could hire a video editor to polish your videos, a graphic designer to create a template for your worksheets, or a VA to create your transcriptions. Yes it will cost more, but it could save you a lot of time and stress.

- **Don't be a perfectionist** – yes you want your content to be good quality, but trying to make it perfect right from the get go is a sure fire way to end up falling behind and stressing yourself out. As the saying goes 'don't get it perfect, just get it going' – as long as it's useful to your members then that's fine – you can always polish things later if you want to.

Day Eleven: Action Steps

1. **Start using the quick and easy content planning sheet** on the next page to plan out your content

2. **Think about any additional tools or software you might need** to invest in and do your research into the best options.

Your Content Planner

Use the below worksheet to plan your content. You can replicate this worksheet for each piece of content you will be creating if needed (for example for each module if it is a course).

Content Description

What is this content all about? Why do they need to know this?

Content Outcomes

What will a member achieve after going through this content? What will they learn?

Methodology

How will these outcomes be accomplished? What practical steps need to be taken? What process needs to be followed? (this forms the core of what you're teaching and will include you providing how-to guidance, tutorials, walkthrough etc)

Objection Handling

What likely objections may students have? Which "what-if...?" scenarios could they present? (i.e. "What if I can't afford the equipment you recommend?") How will you address those?

Action Steps

Will there be any action steps for members as part of this content? What activities/ exercises will you provide to reinforce what they've learned?

Delivery Mechanism

What kind of content is this?

☐ Workbook   ☐ Course

☐ Tutorial   ☐ Other:

☐ Webinar

_____

Content Format

How are you going to create this content?

☐ Video   ☐ Image/Graphical

☐ Text   ☐ Other:

☐ Audio

_____

Getting Paid

It's probably a fair guess that you want your membership site to make money, and in order to do that you need to have a secure way of taking peoples payment details. There are a variety of options for doing that, and we're going to take a look at these today so that you can make the best choice for your membership site.

Payment Options:

- **PayPal Standard** – the simplest and easiest solution to get started with and well trusted amongst purchasers, but users are taken away from your site to pay.
- **PayPal Pro** – the paid version of PayPal allows members to pay on your site with their credit card. It looks a lot slicker and offers you more protection, but you'll need to put security processes in place to keep payments safe.
- **Stripe** – a great alternative to PayPal and easy to get started with. Purchasers essentially stay on site but the security risk is minimal.
- **Clickbank** – a good option if you want to make use of their affiliate system, but for just taking payments it's unwieldy and expensive and each product needs approval.
- **Merchant Solutions** such as Authorize.net – more effort to set up and you'll need to jump through some hoops and likely become PCI compliant in order to take payments on your site, but you'll have more advanced features and better payment protection.
- **Ecommerce system** such as Woocommerce, 1Shopping Cart or iThemes Exchange – you will still need an actual payment processor like PayPal or Stripe as well with these options. However, they're useful if you want to sell a variety of products, not just memberships.

- **Shopping Cart** such as Zaxaa or SamCart – you'll still need to integrate with PayPal or Stripe for taking payments, however they often offer more advanced features like one-click upsells.

Our personal preference when starting out tends to be PayPal or Stripe. Most membership plugins will integrate with these (some may require an add-on for Stripe) and you can get your account set up quickly and easily. The Stripe checkout process is nicer than PayPal's (unless using PayPal Pro) as it creates a more cohesive feel and Stripe will also store your users card details, making future payments easier.

It can be a good idea to still offer a PayPal option even when using Stripe though as many of your potential members will already have a PayPal account that they like to use for payments. There is also an element of trust with PayPal that isn't necessarily there when taking payments on your own site.

Some things to consider when choosing a payment processing option:

- **Security** – if you're taking any payment details on your actual membership site, rather than routing someone to an external service like PayPal, you need to make sure your website is super secure. If you're using Stripe then getting an SSL certificate for your website (this can be done through your hosting company) may be all you need, but for PayPal Pro or most merchant systems you may need to jump through more hoops and become fully PCI compliant. Make sure when selecting your payment processor that you do your homework and know exactly what security you need to put in place to take payments through them safely.

- **Integrations** – if the aim is to build a membership site it makes sense to choose a payment processor that will integrate with the membership plugin you decide to use. PayPal (standard and Pro) and Stripe are the commonest options here, but Clickbank and Authorize.net are common integrations too. For other payment options you would need to check what membership integrations are possible.
- **Income** – how much are you likely to get paid each month? If you're looking at making 5+ figures a month then standard PayPal isn't a good choice. You'd want something more robust like PayPal Pro, Authorize.net or another merchant account, ideally with a dedicated account manager or support service.
- **Fees** – each payment system has different fees, either a percentage of your income or a flat monthly fee, or both. Make sure you're aware of exactly what you'll be giving them and any possible additions or increases (for example PayPal Pro requires an additional monthly fee if you want to take recurring payments).
- **Recurring payments** – if you want to take recurring payments or instalments, make sure you have this option with your chosen payment method. For example with WooCommerce, you would need to purchase an additional add-on (Woo Subscriptions) in order to do this.

Day Twelve: Action Steps

1. **Research the different payment options** listed above and select which you would like to use, then set up your account.

Staying in Touch With Members

The last piece of the puzzle that we need to put together before we decide on our membership plugin and start building our site is the email marketing system that we're going to use.

Aside from any community element that you have for your site, your email list will be your main way of communicating with members about their membership, so it's an important piece of the puzzle – you might want to email members a weekly roundup of what's been going on in the membership for example.

Now, you've actually probably already got an email marketing system that you're using for your wait list and any other marketing activity you're doing. If you're happy with your current set up then that's great, take a day off!

However, it's worth making sure that you're using the right system for your needs before you start enrolling members.

Things to consider:

- **Integrations** – most membership plugins will automatically add members to a mailing list that you select, keeping the sign-up process nice and easy. However, each membership system has different integration options so your choice of email service may affect the membership options available to you.
- **Automations** – are you going to want to make use of more advanced marketing automation at any point? The automation capabilities vary between provider with Aweber and Mailchimp offering more basic options and ActiveCampaign and Infusionsoft offering some much more advanced (and really clever) options.

- **Cost** – how much are you prepared to pay? We don't actually think you need to go for the most expensive option at all, but to use your email system effectively you are likely going to need to pay something, even if it's just $10 a month.
- **Future Needs** – what are you likely to need in the future? If you have Infusionsoft or Ontraport on your 'must have for the future' list then you might want to consider using them from the start. Moving provider, especially to one of these big boys, can be disruptive, especially when a membership site is involved.

The most common email marketing options at the moment are Mailchimp, Aweber and Get Response and pretty much all membership plugins will integrate with these three.

ActiveCampaign is our personal favourite system as it has automation capabilities to rival Infusionsoft, but with a nicer interface and a price point more on par with Mailchimp.

ActiveCampaign is still quite new however, so whilst most of the 'main' membership plugins now integrate with it it's not yet as common as Mailchimp or Aweber so does reduce options somewhat.

There are other options out there too like MadMimi and Constant Contact, however membership integration options are extremely limited for these so we don't really recommend them for membership sites.

If you're already using an option not listed here and don't want to change then, if you can't find a membership plugin that will integrate, you could look at using Zapier to add members to your list instead.

If you're looking to use Infusionsoft or Ontraport, which are more advanced systems combining email marketing, CRM and ecommerce, then this will also affect your membership options.

Ontraport actually has its own membership plugin (though it's not very robust) and there are some additional plugins that will integrate with it too.

Similarly there are several membership plugins that work with Infusionsoft, but if you're going down this route we highly recommend choosing one of the membership systems dedicated just to Infusionsoft in order to get the best results (iMember 360, CustomerHub, Memberium and AccessAlly).

Day Thirteen: Action Steps

1. **Assess your current email marketing system** and whether you are happy to continue using this.

2. **If the answer to the above is no or not sure**, then consider the alternatives and see if there is an option that is a better fit for your needs.

Try them out if you want to see what works for you – you can create a free account at Mailchimp and ActiveCampaign offers a free trial too.

3. **Make a final decision on what you will use**, and if you need to, set up your account.

DAY 14

Choosing a Membership Plugin

Often the first question people ask when they decide to create a membership site is 'what WordPress membership plugin should I use?', which is of course an important question.

However, our response is usually 'what do you need it to do?' rather than a specific answer (and we've been known to silently rage at people blindly recommending membership plugins without any thought to that persons specific needs).

That's the exact same reason we've waited until now to discuss the subject with you – as you've now seen, there's so many different types of membership sites that you can create, so many different features you might want, so many different tools you might need to integrate, that there is no 'one membership plugin to rule them all'.

A great plugin for someone else could be terrible for you.

What you need to consider to make your choice

Every membership plugin will protect your content (as that's their main purpose after all!) but otherwise the feature sets can vary hugely from plugin to plugin.

To ensure you get the best fit for you, consider the following factors:

- **Required features** – look back at your list from day 5. Whilst not all of these features will be part of your actual membership plugin, your aim is to ensure that your chosen plugin will either provide, protect or integrate with all of the options that you need. (Heads up, if you want a more 'course like' structure then we're going to be taking a look at course plugins tomorrow, which you may want to use combined with (or possibly instead of) a membership plugin to get some of your desired features).

- **Integrations** – linked to the above, look at the specific tools you're planning to use (your payment processor, your email system, your forum software etc) and make sure that you factor this into your plugin choice. Yes, you can do some cool stuff with Zapier and API integrations these days, but why mess around with that if you don't have to?

- **Content dripping** – do you need to drip content out regularly? Not all membership plugins provide an easy way to do this. And if you want your content dripping to start on a specific day, rather than time since registration (the traditional content dripping method), then your selection is more limited (think Wishlist, MemberPress and DAP).

- **Ease of use** – some membership plugins are easier than others so where possible pick an option that will be easy for you to maintain at your skill level. We personally love s2Member for example, but don't tend to recommend it unless you're fairly tech savvy.

- **Multiple products** – do you want to be able to sell multiple memberships or products and for people to be able to purchase more than one? Not all membership plugins are capable of what's called 'concurrent memberships' so even if this is something you want in the future rather than straight away, plan ahead.

- **Future proofing** – as mentioned above, plan ahead and think about your future needs as well. If you don't want a forum right now but think you'll add one as a 'phase 2' feature, then don't pick a plugin that doesn't work with forums. If you think you'll need an affiliate system in the future, choose an option that offers this integration. And so on…

- **Tech requirements** – does the plugin have any specific hosting or tech requirements? Some may need your host to have specific software installed, some are only suitable for a new domain (or subdomain), some may require you to increase your hosting package. Check for any specific requirements and make sure you can meet them.

- **Cost** – most membership plugins will have some cost attached to them – the most standard being a one-off fee plus an annual fee if you want to continue receiving updates after the first 12 months (recommended!). There are monthly options and free options too, but bear in mind that for the free options you'll often still need to pay for support or for add-ons to perform specific functions, so it's often not entirely free in the long run. When it comes to cost, it's definitely not a case of 'the more expensive the better', but if your membership site is going to be a business, you should be happy to pay for the software that will be the backbone of it (even if you're just paying for support).

The work we've done so far and the factors above should help you in narrowing down your plugin choice. But, as there are well over 40 different options out there, going through them all to see what will work for you can undoubtedly be a little daunting!

It's not realistic for anyone to go through all those different options, so to help with this we've created our own shortlist of the most common and most reliable options and turned this into a comparison chart that you can download from *www.themembershipguys.com/plugin-comparison* and use to help narrow down your choice.

If you're using Infusionsoft...

We've mentioned previously that if you're using Infusionsoft we really recommend you use an Infusionsoft specific membership plugin in order to get the best features. We haven't included these on our chart as they are much more specialist, but your main options are: iMember 360, CustomerHub, Memberium and Access Ally.

And if you don't want to use WordPress at all...

We work with WordPress and we happen to think this gives you the most flexible options for a membership site.

However, we know that sometimes you just want to get something up and running quickly and easily, and in those instances a hosted solution can be a better option. We're not going to go into the ins and outs of these here, but there's a lot of options for you to choose from, including Kajabi, ValueAddon, Rainmaker, Fedora, Thinkific and even Udemy.

Day Fourteen: Action Steps

1. **Download our plugin comparison chart** and narrow down your choice to 2-3 options.

2. **Take a closer look at the official websites for each of your options and make a final choice** (if you need clarification on features, functionality etc you can usually contact each plugins customer support team with questions).

A Closer Look at Course Plugins

When we looked at choosing a membership plugin yesterday, we mentioned that if you're running a course based membership site then you might want (or need) to also consider an LMS (learning management system) plugin as well as, or in some cases instead of, a membership plugin.

So, as courses are one of the most popular membership types, we're going to take a closer look at LMS plugins today.

Why would you need a separate course plugin?

Well, courses often have specific needs that other types of membership site don't.

Typically there will be a set structure to the course (usually modules broken down into lessons) that you want members to progress through in a specific order. You may also want to add in some kind of quiz or assessment either at the end of the course or as part of each module. And you may even require the ability for members to complete and upload 'homework' that you can assess.

It may also be more important with a course to have an easy way for members to keep track of course progress, and also for you to be able to see the progress your members are making.

You may want to provide a certificate of completion to your members once they finish the course.

And if you're offering multiple courses then you might want to set up pre-requisites and create a complete learning pathway, not to mention have an easy way to keep each of those courses separate and distinguished.

Essentially, a course is often more feature rich, and needs more than just content protection. Which is where an LMS or course specific plugin comes in handy.

However, it's also perfectly fine to run a course without any additional bells and whistles, so running a course doesn't necessarily need a separate plugin at all. As with so many things to do with membership sites – it comes down to what your specific needs for your site actually are.

What are the differences between membership plugins and LMS plugins?

If you're sat there wondering what the specific differences are between an LMS (course) plugin and a membership plugin then don't worry, you're not alone. It can definitely get a bit confusing.

At it's heart a membership plugin is simply designed to protect your content and control access, although many do a lot more than that too these days.

On the other hand, an LMS plugin is designed to provide a richer course experience for your members.

You could also say a membership plugin takes care of the big picture, whilst an LMS plugin takes care of the finer details, such as:

- Provide a course structure for your content (i.e. modules and lessons)
- Offer quiz and assignment features
- Provide progress tracking for students
- Allow you to see students progress and stats

- Offer completion certificates
- Can be used for multiple courses on one site easily
- Enable the use of pre-requisites for unlocking content
- Protect course content from non-registered users
- May drip content
- May handle payment and registration
- May integrate with forums and gamification options

The main course plugin options:

- **LearnDash** – this plugin packs a powerful punch and offers a whole ton of features. Can be used standalone or integrates with several membership plugins easily (including MemberPress and Wishlist Member).
- **Woo Sensei** – this LMS is designed to work with the other Woo plugins, such as WooCommerce and Woo Subscriptions rather than external membership plugins. So if you're using other Woo plugins it's your best option.
- **WPCourseware** – probably the quickest and easiest option of the three to set up, but not quite as feature rich. You'll need a separate membership plugin, but luckily it integrates with at least 10 of them.
- **LifterLMS** – this is relatively new but it's pretty nifty and has a good feature set. It includes membership protection too so you don't necessarily need an additional plugin.
- **CoursePress** – this is by the folks at WPMU Dev and there is both a free and paid version. It also comes with a pre-styled theme that you can use with it and offers a range of useful features.
- **LearnPress** – the core plugin is free and provides simple

features in an easy to use format. However you can also purchase a number of add-ons for increased functionality.

Some alternatives:

If you're setting up a simple course and don't need all the bells and whistles like quizzes but want an easy way to add a course structure and some progress tracking, then take a look at Thrive Themes. 4 of their themes have a really nifty feature called Apprentice, which you can turn on to create a course.

It's probably the quickest and easiest course option we've seen, but it is a lot more basic than an LMS and you'll still need a membership plugin to protect your content.

Alternatively if you'd prefer not to have the hassle of wrestling with WordPress plugins, then there are some great choices for cloud based course platforms; including Thinkific and Teachable.

Day Fifteen: Action Steps

If you're not setting up a course you can consider yourself action free today! If you are running a course then:

1. **Consider whether you need the additional features of an LMS plugin** or whether your course can run using normal WordPress pages and a membership plugin.

2. Go to *www.themembershipguys.com/course-plugin-chart* to compare the leading WordPress LMS plugins

Choosing a Membership Theme

Before we install our membership plugin, we first need to have a site to install it on! Now, if you're using your current website for your membership site then you will already have this step covered, but if not then today we're going to take a look at how to choose a theme for your membership site.

What do we mean by "theme"?

If you're new to WordPress then this may be new terminology for you, but essentially your theme is the template that your site uses to give it its look and style. It adds the design to your membership plugin's functionality.

Now, some membership plugins do come with their own theme, like OptimizePress, Access Ally and Paid Memberships Pro; but most don't – they're all about functionality not style.

So, unless you're using an option with a theme you will need to install your own theme for your site.

Things to consider when choosing a theme:

- **Style** – what kind of website styles do you like? Take a look at some of your favourite sites, especially those that are similar to what you're planning to do and make a note of the features that you like. And, whilst we don't condone copying someone else's site at all, if you want to see what theme they are using for inspiration you could try *www.whatwpthemeisthat.com*.
- **Layout** – what layouts do you need for your membership? If you want to have a lot of flexibility in your page layouts you will want to look for a more feature rich theme, perhaps including a page builder. If you know you want to create a lot of landing

pages (typically pages without a header, footer or sidebar) then look for a theme that includes a landing page template

- **Page builders** – many popular themes (think Divi) include some kind of page builder or visual composer to help make interesting page layouts easy. When you're DIYing your site these can be great, however they can cause issues with some membership plugins, in particular the OptimizePress plugin.

- **Incompatibilities** – when you're dealing with code, in can be inevitable that you will get some clashes. Once you know what membership plugin you will be using have a Google and see if there are any known theme incompatibilities. Many membership plugins will actually have this information somewhere on their website. For most membership plugins there may be one or two potential issues, however if you're planning on using OptimizePress as a plugin, check out this lengthy list first!

- **Responsiveness** – it's almost certain that your visitors and members will try to look at your site on their phone or tablet at some point or another. So, do yourself a favour and make sure that any theme you purchase is already responsive and works well on smaller screens (and then double check its responsiveness once you've actually set it up!).

- **Skill level** – how well versed are you with WordPress? Have you set up a theme before? If you're brand new to this and you don't want to hire any help, look for something that needs the minimum amount of customisation.

- **Support** – choose a theme that has support in place, whether that's a forum, a ticket system or an email. You want to know that if you have a problem with the theme there is someone you can get in touch with to help with the issue.

- **Licensing** - one of the most popular places to purchase WordPress themes is the www.themeforest.net marketplace; however we urge caution when doing so as their licensing rules mean that if you're charging people to join a site that uses their theme (as you would be for your paid membership) then you need their "extended license", which typically costs 10-20 times more than a regular license.

Some themes to consider

There are thousands and thousands of themes out there – we've quite often lost hours of our life looking through different options! So here's a few starting suggestions to narrow things down for you.

There are a ridiculous amount of themes out there and I've quite often lost hours of my life looking through the different options! So here's a few starting suggestions to narrow things down for you.

Great for flexibility:

- Divi (by ElegantThemes.com)
- BeaverBuilder
- OptimizePress

For simplicity:

- Thrive Themes (thrivethemes.com)
- Genesis child theme (studiopress.com)

With Thrive Themes you can also use their content builder plugin to create more complicated page layouts and landing pages, so whilst the themes are a simple option, you can still have a great level of customisability.

For community sites:

- Boss theme (buddyboss.com)

And last but most definitely not least, we created our own theme designed specifically for memberships called *'Memberoni',* which is exclusively available to members of our *Member Site Academy*

There are of course plenty of other themes for you to choose from, these are just a few of our favourites to give you a head start.

Day Sixteen: Action Steps

1. **Using the 'things to consider' as a guide choose a theme** for your membership site(if in doubt look at reviews and testimonials for the theme).

2. **Install and set up your theme** – most good themes come with instructions of how to set them up. You can also usually import demo content to make the theme right, and then switch this content with your own.

Choosing your theme is an important step, and whilst you can change theme at any time it's not ideal to do so, especially when you have members attached to your site. So take some time to look through the features and documentation of your chosen theme.

Setting Up Your Membership Plugin

Here's the part you may have been dreading - we're going to be installing and setting up our membership plugin today!

Although we'll be delving into certain aspects of your membership set up – such as protecting your files, creating your membership dashboard and setting up your welcome email – in more depth over the next few days, we're starting the main plugin set up today.

But don't worry if it feels overwhelming or you're not sure what to do about something specific as it's most likely something we'll be covering later.

You can also jump in the Facebook community at www.talkmemberships.com and ask any questions you might have if you get stuck.

Where to start...

There are so many membership plugins, and each with their own setup process, that providing a 'one-size fits all' membership setup guide is an impossible task.

So we can't give you *really* specific steps to follow today as it will depend on your chosen plugin.

The good news, however, is that every membership plugin comes with its own setup instructions, walkthrough videos and/or user manuals; and many also have a setup wizard that will help you once you have installed and activated the plugin.

So, even if you're the kind of person that usually puts up IKEA flat pack furniture without reading the instructions, we really recommend that in this instance you read/watch and follow them rather than trying to muddle it out by yourself.

Walkthroughs

We're continuously adding set-up walkthrough courses for our members at Member Site Academy (*www.membersiteacademy.com*) – so if you want step-by-step guidance then that's a great resource to start with; however if you're not a member then you can also see some shorter versions of our walkthrough courses on YouTube:

- **MemberPress:** http://tmgys.co/kym-memberpress
- **Wishlist Member:** http://tmgys.co/kym-wishlist
- **OptimizeMember:** http://tmgys.co/kym-optimize

Day Seventeen: Action Steps

1. If you haven't already then **purchase or download your chosen membership plugin**

2. **Use our development checklist** on the next page to keep you on track while setting everything up

3. **Locate the installation/setup instructions for your plugin** or use either our Member Site Academy courses or one of the 3 free walkthroughs we provided above.

4. **Get stuck in and install your chosen plugin!** Follow their set up guidelines for completing the general settings and installing your payment processor and email marketing service.

Initial Development Checklist

Use the following checklist to ensure you don't miss anything whilst setting up your site and installing your membership plugin.

Initial Configuration

- ☐ Set up web hosting for your chosen domain name
- ☐ Have your hosting provider install an SSL certificate (if required)
- ☐ Install WordPress on your hosting
- ☐ Set up a coming soon plugin or landing page while your website is being developed

Theme Setup

- ☐ Install your chosen theme
    - ☐ Customize with your logo, brand colours and fonts
    - ☐ Create any page layouts that you need
- ☐ Create any front-end (non-member) pages needed, such as:
    - ☐ Homepage
    - ☐ About page
    - ☐ Contact page
    - ☐ Blog
    - ☐ FAQs
    - ☐ Opt-in page
- ☐ Create your website menu (Appearance > Menus)
- ☐ If you want a different menu for guests and logged in members, use a plugin like Nav Menu Roles (https://wordpress.org/plugins/nav-menu-roles/) to achieve this

Membership Plugin Setup

- ☐ Install your membership plugin
    - ☐ Add your license key (if required)
- ☐ Set up your membership plugin:
    - ☐ Complete the general plugin settings
    - ☐ Integrate your payment processor
    - ☐ Integrate your email marketing service
    - ☐ Create your membership levels
    - ☐ Customize your membership confirmation/welcome email
- ☐ Install and setup your LMS plugin (if required)
    - ☐ Create your course structure
    - ☐ Setup and quizzes or other course functions

A Look At Video Content

Many membership sites will include at least some video content, so today we're going to focus on this a little more.

Where to store your video content

There are a variety of affordable options available for video hosting these days, with YouTube undoubtedly being the most well known.

However, YouTube, whilst great for free content, is most definitely not a recommended option for membership videos. Yes, you can set videos to be 'unlisted', but this doesn't stop them from being found or shared, and do you want your members paying for content that they could find for free?

So, making sure your videos are secure and can't be watched by non-members is paramount when creating a paid site.

The main options we recommend:

- **Vimeo Pro** – Vimeo provides solid video hosting and you can select which domain names your videos are watchable from, whether or not they can be downloaded, add custom thumbnails and set your player styling.

  It's a yearly fee, but it's lower cost than Wistia and worth it for the increased protection and features.

- **Wistia** – Wistia provides great video quality, useful analytic features (want to see at what point people stop watching a video? No problem!) and a highly customisable video player. You can also protect your videos by domain name, create playlists, add calls-to-action and prevent downloads, making it both highly customisable and secure. All these features come at a cost though.

- **Amazon s3** – you can also upload your video files to Amazon's file storage system. This is the cheapest hosting method available (you'll be charged based on the amount of space used) but it does have its drawbacks.

   Namely that you will need to install a third party video player plugin, such as s3 Media Maestro or JW Player, onto your WordPress site in order for your video files to be watchable. So, it's a little bit more effort to set up than the other options.

You can't really go wrong with any of these options, so it's mainly a case of picking the one that feels best to you. And sticking with it so that all your on-site videos are consistent.

We personally use Vimeo for all of our membership content inside Member Site Academy.

Adding your videos to your membership site

Once you've uploaded your files to your chosen host, you also need to add them to your membership site.

With both Vimeo and Wistia you'll be able to get an embed code for each video, which you would then paste into the relevant place on your site (in the 'text' view of your WordPress editing screen).

You may need to adjust the size but otherwise your videos should be good to go straight away (just make sure you've set the privacy settings and customised your player in the relevant Vimeo/Wistia settings).

For Amazon s3 then, as mentioned above, you would first need to install an s3 video player plugin to your site.

Each of these works slightly differently, but once installed you should be able to add a link to your Amazon s3 video file to any page on your site.

In this instance Amazon s3 won't have any influence on player style, video size or analytics – this would all be done by your video player plugin.

As well as protecting your video file on the hosting side, also be sure to use your membership plugins settings to protect any of your website pages that have your member videos on.

This way non-members can't see your videos by accident, and your members also can't share them.

Should your videos be downloadable?

To a large extent this is up to you and also the type of site you are running.

Many people like to download videos to watch when they are offline and certain types of videos, such as fitness workouts, are particularly likely for members to want to download.

However, for courses or educational content it's less common for videos to be downloadable.

The main cons of your videos being downloadable are that members could 'download and run' and they could also share your content with non-members, which we obviously don't want (however, if someone really wanted to share your content, they'd find a way to do it whether your videos are downloadable or not!).

If you don't want to make your videos downloadable, then depending on the content you may want to make the corresponding slides downloadable (if it's a PowerPoint or Keynote video) or strip the audio from the video and make this downloadable as an mp3 for members to listen to offline instead

Day Eighteen: Action Steps

1. **Decide on your video hosting solution** – check out the official websites of both vimeo.com and wistia.com to see how they compare.

2. **Set up your account** and, when ready, start uploading your video content

Protecting Files & Downloads

Yesterday we looked at your video content and today we're going to take a look at your other membership files, such as PDFs and audio mp3's, and how you can store them safely and securely.

As with videos, we want to ensure that non-members can't access your membership files, but there's also another reason we need to look at downloadable files: size.

PDFs, audio files, word documents etc all take up varying degrees of space and, unless you have a dedicated server or some other super duper hosting, you likely have limited storage available.

While that space might be enough to upload your files, doing so is likely to cause performance/speed issues for your site – and we don't want your members complaining that your site is loading too slowly!

The solution?

Using off-site file storage for your membership files. This allows you to add download links to your site for each file without it taking space on your server. It can also be easier to keep your files secure, as there is less risk of them appearing in Google or other search engines.

There's a variety of cloud storage solutions that you could use, including Dropbox and Google Drive, however our preference is Amazon S3 storage. It's low cost, secure, easy to use, and many membership plugins will offer protection for your Amazon S3 files.

Using your membership plugins file protection features

Having said that, if you're just offering a few small PDF files for download, you may just want to add them directly to your site. If this is the case then your first step is to check the file protection that your membership plugin offers.

Each plugin does this differently (and some might not include it – in which case definitely use an external solution).

For example with MemberPress you would simply upload your document via the WordPress media function, copy the resulting URL and then create a MemberPress rule protecting that URL. For Wishlist Member on the other hand you could create a private folder on your hosting, add any downloads to this and then protect the whole folder in the Wishlist content settings.

Audio files

For audio files you may want to allow these to be streamed online as well as downloaded, in which case you could use something like SoundCloud to host the files, use a podcasting plugin or, if using Amazon S3 storage many of the media players available for playing s3 video files will also play audio files stored there.

Day Nineteen: Action Steps

1. **Watch our video on setting up Amazon S3** storage and protecting your download links at *http://tmgys.co/kym-amazon*

2. **Set up your Amazon S3 account** and upload your files if you already have them ready.

3. **Not using Amazon S3?** Set up you chosen method instead.

DAY 20

Adding Your Membership Content

We've looked at your video content and downloads and now it's time to look at adding your on page content.

To a certain degree this will depend on the theme that you're using, so we're not going to look too much at layout here, except to say to keep it simple and try not to add too many elements to a page.

The aim is to make it clear what a member needs to do whenever they land on a page – do they need to watch a video, download a file, read some text?

If you're offering accompanying downloads, make it clear what each is, and if there's anything they need to take action on, make this clear too.

Some things to consider:

- **Page hierarchy** – take advantage of the inbuilt WordPress Parent-Child page hierarchy for keeping your membership pages in check (if you're not familiar with WordPress, you can create what is known as Parent and Child pages). For example you may create your member dashboard as a parent page, and then add your module pages as child pages under this, with your lesson pages as child pages of your module page. Your URL for a page like this would then be yourdomain.com/dashboard/module-1/lesson-1 (for example). This kind of structure not only makes it easier for you to keep your pages organised and your sitemap clear, but it can make page protection easier with certain membership plugins too.
- **Text Formatting** – make sure any text on your page is easily legible. These days that means using at least a 14px font size.

For paragraphs of text use a standard serif or sans serif font, not a fancy script or handwritten font. Also make sure your font colour is easily readable (try on a variety of devices, including your phone), grey is a common colour for paragraph text but make it too pale and it becomes difficult to read on a bright screen! Also make use of header text to break up your paragraphs and make it easier to scan read your content.

- **Content Flow** – have a logical flow to your content, both on an individual page and overall. You should have a good idea of your page flow from the sitemap you created on day 7, but make sure this still makes sense. For on page content, it's common to have your most important content first, such as a video, followed by accompanying text or a download button for any files. Avoid putting too many videos on one page side by side, as it can appear overwhelming.

- **Tags & Categories** – as well as creating your membership content as pages, you may also want to create some content as posts on your site (like you would create a blog post). This can be useful for premium content sites where you're essentially going to be producing lots of ongoing content on various topics – you can then use the category feature that posts have to help you organise your content.

- **Navigation Menus** – how will your members move between your content? Make sure that your pages aren't 'out in the wild' and are easily findable. The last thing you want is to have a site packed full of awesome content that your members don't even know exists!

And don't forget to protect your content!

It goes without saying that any page you create for your membership content, you need to protect via your membership plugin settings.

The way in which protection is handled will differ according to the plugin you're using; so refer back to their documentation for a reminder on how to do this.

When you're busy adding lots of content it can be easy to forget this crucial step, so make sure you set up a system that reminds you to do this – some plugins allow you to add your content protection on the page itself as you create it, and others require you to set the protection through their plugin settings.

Day Twenty: Action Steps

1. **Think about how you want your membership content to be laid out on the page.** Do you need more than one page layout? We find sketching it out first really helps.

2. **If your content is ready, start adding this to your site.**

3. **Make sure to protect any content** that you add!

4. **Create a navigation menu** for your main pages so that they are easy to get to.

To Drip or Not to Drip...

We looked at adding your content yesterday, but there's an additional feature you may need to set up in order to get your membership content working as you'd like – 'drip feeding'.

What is drip feeding and why might you use it?

Drip feeding is essentially time-releasing your content so that it isn't all available immediately. But unlike simply providing ongoing content (where members get the same content each month regardless of when they joined), your content is released on a set schedule based, usually, on when the member signed up.

This kind of content release can be a good way of preventing 'download and run' members who join your site, download all your content and then cancel straight away.

For monthly membership sites it's a good way of delivering new content each month so that members want to stay. It's also a good way of avoiding overwhelm if you're providing a lot of information – particularly for online courses.

How to drip feed your content

There are two main ways that you could drip feed your content.

The most typical method is based on time since registration. In this instance your content is set to release a set number of days after a member joins – this could be 7 days, 30 days, 90 days, whatever you prefer.

Every member who joins will get access to that content on the specified day of their membership, regardless of when they joined. So a member joining in June would receive the same content on day 7 as a member joining in February did.

The other method works based on the first piece of content being released on a set date. So say, for example, that you are running a course and you want it to start on September 1st, but you want members to be able to join any time between now and that date.

You couldn't use the traditional content dripping method to achieve this as your members would all have joined at different times. However, what you can do is set your first module to be released on the 1st September, and then the next module 7 days (or 30 etc) after that.

So your members all receive exactly the same content on exactly the same day, even though they joined at different times. At the moment only certain membership plugins support this type of content drip though (Wishlist, MemberPress and DAP being the main 3).

How you actually set up your drip feed will depend on your membership plugin. However it's important to note that not all membership plugins offer a content dripping option.

Whilst each plugin will have a different way of setting up your content drip, they will usually explain how in their set up instructions.

Some plugins do it as part of their content protection (for example with MemberPress and DAP you set the drip schedule when you create your protection rules), some offer a shortcode that you wrap around the content you want dripped (s2Member).

Others provide an option to set the drip settings on your actual content creation page (OptimizeMember) and Wishlist uses a process called 'Sequential Upgrade' requiring you to create a new membership level for each time you want new content to be released.

One last thing...

Often the dripped content is added to a members account automatically behind the scenes or when they next login.

However, if this process isn't working effectively (your new content isn't being given to members when it should be) you may need to setup what is called a 'cron job' on your hosting – this tells your site to perform certain tasks automatically at certain times. The main membership plugin where you may need to set this up is Wishlist.

Day Twenty-One: Action Steps

1. **Decide whether you want to drip feed your content.** If so, work out your schedule and refer to your plugin documentation to see how to apply this to your membership content.

2. **Don't want to drip feed your content?** You get to take today off, do something fun!

Creating Your Essential Membership Pages

In all the excitement to get your membership site content up and running, it can be easy to forget the essential system pages that your membership site also needs.

So today we're going to take a brief look at these pages so that you can make sure you've got it covered.

What pages do you need?

You will generally need the following:

- **Registration page** – this will usually be created by your membership plugin, but if you can it's a good idea to customise this. You may want to add some text reminding them of what they get when they sign-up for example, or add in a terms of service checkbox or other custom field (for example their location).

- **Thank you page** – this is the page people go to after registering and paying, so it's important to welcome them, thank them for joining and let them know the next steps. Can they log straight in? Do they need to check their emails? When do they get access to their content? You could even put a video on this page if you wanted to make it even more personal.

- **Login page** – there's 3 options for this depending on your plugin: 1. It uses the default WordPress login, 2. It creates its own login page, 3. It gives you a widget or shortcode that you can place on your site wherever you want a login form. As with the registration page we recommend you customise the login if you can – either by styling your default WordPress login (you could use a plugin like Theme My Login for this) or the page that your membership plugin has created. It's also a good idea to add a link on your login to your sales page, for people who aren't yet members.

- **Member Dashboard** – this is the first page that your members will see when they login, and as such is important both for their initial welcome and for their ongoing use. What you have on your dashboard depends on your site, but we will be looking at this more in-depth tomorrow. You'll normally need to create this page yourself and then set it as the dashboard/welcome/after-login page in your membership plugin settings.

- **Account page** – this page will usually be created by your membership plugin, or they may provide a shortcode for you to add to your own page. Account pages will typically be where members can see their subscriptions and change details such as their password (it may include billing and cancellation options as well). Not all membership plugins will have an account page so don't worry if yours doesn't.

- **Profile page** – at a minimum this will be the standard WordPress profile where a user can change their password. Many membership plugins will offer a specific profile page to avoid members having to go to that default WP profile (it may also be part of the account page above though). Unless you're using a plugin like BuddyPress or a Member Directory plugin the profile will usually only be seen by the individual member.

- **Support page** – we recommend you create this page to give details of how members can get support if needed. It may include a contact form, support contact details, links to a customer ticket system or however you prefer to receive support requests from members (you could even use a live chat plugin if you wanted to).

The purpose of this page is to make it easy for members to get in touch if they need to, and it's particularly important if you need to manually cancel member accounts.

- **Cancellation page** – if your members can cancel their own accounts then you'll need a page allowing them to do this (unless it's part of their account page). It can be good to personalise this and provide some reasons why they might not want to cancel too!

Don't forget the legalities!

You're also going to need certain legal pages on your site – what exactly you need will depend on your country, so you may want to consult an attorney (or the mighty Google!), but you can also get things like 'Terms & Conditions' templates online.

At the very least you will need a privacy policy and a terms of service page, but possibly also a disclaimer.

We typically recommend putting the links to these pages as a menu in your footer (where your copyright is) rather than in your main navigation.

However, you may also want to consider whether you put a check box on your registration page so that members have to specify that they have read your terms before joining.

If you're offering any kind of refund policy make sure the details of this are covered in your legal pages – specify under what circumstances the refund will be offered and how it can be requested. Similarly, if you're offering a trial, make sure the terms of this are clear – will you automatically take payment at the end of the trial unless they cancel? Will you send them a reminder that their trial is ending?

Whilst the chances of any issues occurring are minimal, it's always best to make sure you've got your legal ducks in a row from the start!

Day Twenty-Two: Action Steps

1. **See which of the above pages are available with your membership plugin** and which you need/want to create yourself.

2. **Customise any pages** that your plugin creates for you (if possible).

3. **Create the additional pages** that you need and make sure they will be easily accessible to your members.

Developing Your Member Dashboard

We looked at your membership pages yesterday, and today we're going to take a closer look at your membership dashboard, which is sometimes referred to as the "welcome page".

Typically your dashboard is the page that members are taken to whenever they log in to your site, so it's prime real estate and you want to make sure that it's working for you and for your members.

At its simplest your dashboard needs to provide easy access to anything that your members might need – for example links to their course content.

More complex dashboards can be a source of news, latest content, latest forum posts and even additional upgrade/upsell content.

What to include

What you include on your dashboard will depend to a large extent on the type of membership site you're creating. For a course website you may just want to provide links to each of your course modules, or for a multi-course site you may want to add links to each course. For sites with a variety of different content, you'll probably want to make sure that each section of the site is accessible from the dashboard.

Essentially, the more complex your site is, the more you might need to include on your dashboard.

Some common dashboard inclusions:

- **Welcome video or walkthrough** of how to use the site (if they're likely to only watch this once, it might be better suited to the thank you page or your onboarding sequence).

- **Access to your course modules** or direct access to your course content.
- **Contact form for support**, feedback or questions (or a clear link for contact/support).
- **Link to profile or account**, or have these details displayed on the page itself.
- **Details of any live trainings/calls** and how they can be registered for (or even a link to add to calendar).
- **Access to your community**, whether this is on-site or off (if using something like Facebook make sure your link is set to open in a new tab so they don't leave your main site).
- For sites selling multiple products you may want to include **access to all your products on one dashboard**, with ones the member doesn't have access to going to a sales page (a great way to upsell without trying!)
- For sites with a forum you may want to include a **'latest discussions' section** to entice people to spend time in the community (how easy this is depends on your forum software!).
- **Details of your latest content** if new content is being added regularly. For sites with ongoing content being released it's beneficial to keep the dashboard fresh.
- An area for **announcements** or important information.
- For a site with varying types of content then a **link to each of the main content areas** (i.e. courses, calls, resources, downloads etc).
- If using an LMS plugin you can often embed a **course outline** with all the modules and lessons available.
- If offering a course with progress tracking you could enable people to **pick up where they left off** from the dashboard.

You don't want your dashboard to be overwhelming, so don't feel like you have to link to everything on your site here, but definitely make sure any key areas are clear and accessible (with other less important links elsewhere in your navigation).

Making the dashboard visual, for example using graphics instead of just text, is a great way to give this first page impact – although it's important to make sure the style is still in keeping with the rest of your site.

The way that you actually put your dashboard together will depend on the plugins and theme that you're using. Many plugins will include widgets or shortcodes that enable you to tinker with the layout and make things look pretty. Even if yours don't simply creating graphics to use for buttons leading to all your key sections is often enough.

Dashboard examples

We've put together examples of some great membership site dashboards, with a breakdown of what makes them work well at *www.tmgys.co/kym-dashboards*

Day Twenty-Three: Action Steps

1. **Decide on the key content** you will add to your dashboard

2. **Create any relevant graphics** or icons (Canva or PicMonkey are great tools for this)

3. **Start creating your dashboard!**

Building Anticipation and Buzz

Our focus has been on actually building your membership site lately, but it's important not to forget about your pre-launch marketing.

Now is the time that you want to start increasing anticipation for your launch, piquing people's interest and putting out some teasers of what's coming up. It's time to build some buzz!

On day 3 of the challenge we first looked at launch plans and if you did your homework then you will have come up with some pre-launch activities.

Since then you've created a more comprehensive plan for your membership site, so you should now have a much clearer idea of what you're actually promoting. And now, when we're on the cusp of finishing our actual site build, is the perfect time to use that additional information to ramp things up a bit.

Some things you could do:

- **Take a screenshot of your new dashboard** and post it on social media with a teasing headline about what you're building (and a link to your waitlist!).
- **Start releasing more details** of what you're going to be offering – we're talking snippets here, not the full shebang (you want to create some mystery and anticipation!).
- **Provide some behind-the-scenes content** on social media and your blog.
- **Share in Facebook groups** and other online groups what you're working on and your launch date.
- **Double your efforts to grow your audience!** Start thinking about running some Facebook ads to a piece of relevant

content that promotes your upcoming site and waitlist.

- **Consider fleshing out your waitlist landing page** into a mini-sales page with more information about what your site will contain.
- **Reach out to any possible advocates** and ask them to help spread the word.
- **Start guest posting** or arrange some interviews or podcast discussions.
- **Consider running a contest or giveaway** to grow your list as well as get people excited and looking forward to your launch.
- Make sure any blog content etc that you're putting out is relevant to your upcoming site.
- **Start a countdown** on your waitlist landing page if there isn't one already.
- **Make a video** talking about the upcoming launch.
- **Get creative** – what could you do to make you stand out? How could you use different content delivery to get people talking?

Discounts and Bonuses

At this point you also want to be thinking about whether you're going to offer any special deals for your launch, such as price discounts or bonuses.

It's usually a good idea to create some early bird pricing for your waitlist subscribers at a minimum, although it's customary to offer some launch deals to everyone else as well.

How big a discount you want to offer is up to you, but it's a good idea to make it significant enough to matter – something like 25% off monthly pricing or 30% off one-off pricing.

Bonuses can be used in addition to or instead of discounts and are a great way of both rewarding people for jumping on board and also nudging people off the fence.

If your site is going to be evergreen (open permanently) bonuses are a good way of creating scarcity that can otherwise be lacking, so be sure to have several bonuses up your sleeve to use at different points.

If your site is time sensitive then scarcity/urgency is less of an issue, but bonuses can still be useful to entice and sweeten the deal, as well as to encourage sign-ups straight away rather than at the eleventh hour.

Day Twenty-Four: Action Steps

1. **Start ramping up your pre-launch marketing** – take a look at the suggestions above and see what you can add in to your plan.

2. **Think about what bonuses you could provide** – products you've already created (that are relevant!), exclusive training or even 1-2-1 access to you work well.

3. **Think about your launch pricing** – what discounts and early bird pricing could you offer?

DAY 25

Setting Up Your Community

We're back to building our site today and we're going to take a brief look at setting up the community aspect of your site.

Now, we talked about the value of adding a community to your site back on day 8, so you should already know what you're planning to offer here.

How you actually set up your community depends on your chosen tools, but here are some suggestions and guidelines:

Comments System – if you'd just like members to be able to comment directly on your content then you can use the default WordPress comment system for this. Members will already be logged into your site so won't need to jump through any hoops in order to leave a comment. You could also use Facebook comments as an alternative. If doing that you might find this plugin helpful: https://wordpress.org/plugins/facebook-comments-plugin/

Be sure to actually check the comments on your pages and respond to any that require it!

WP forum (i.e. bbPress) – you'll install this like any other plugin on your site. For bbPress once installed you can select a number of options and then you can create your forums and categories and customize as needed. It works great with BuddyPress for additional features like private messaging and there are a lot of plugins to enhance bbPress features if you need a little more than it provides out of the box (such as https://wordpress.org/plugins/buddypress-media/).

Make sure when you install bbPress (or similar) that you protect any pages that it uses via your membership plugin – it can be easy to forget and leave your forum open to viewing by non-members!

Social media group (Facebook, Slack, Google+, LinkedIn) – creating your group on your chosen channel should be easy to do. Make sure you give it a name that links it to your membership and also make sure you have something in place that means that non-members can't join. This may need to be manual checks via the users name or email address – in which case make this clear somewhere on your site.

Typically once your group is set up you can simply add a link to this in your membership site (the dashboard is a great place for this, as well as your main navigation) to allow easy access. As members will need to sign up to the group separately it's also a good idea to include the sign-up link in your welcome email.

Forum software – how you set this up will depend on which software you're using, but usually the software is installed on a sub-folder or sub-domain of your site, so it isn't actually part of your main membership site at all.

The main issue with using forum software is therefore bridging it with your main membership site as ideally you don't want members to have a separate login for your forum! If you're using something like Vanilla Forums or phpBB then there are plugins available to integrate with WordPress, or for something like IP.Board (which is what we use) there is a third-party bridging plugin which enables single-sign-on (SSO).

Office hours /Q & A sessions – a popular way of offering these kind of sessions is via Google Hangouts, which can simply be embedded on a (protected) page on your website in order for people to watch live. You can then add a recording of the session on an archive page of your site for people who weren't able to attend. Zoom or GoToWebinar are good alternatives.

If you'd like to accept comments from members during the session then you can also embed ChatWING or Chatroll in order to do this.

No community – make sure that you have a contact link on your site, or a support form, so that a member can get in touch with you with any questions. You may also want to make it clear the level of support provided (e.g. that you'll get back to them within 48 hours etc).

If you're not offering a community but you are providing 1-2-1 support then give clear details on how this support is accessed – do they need to book a call via your scheduling service? If so embed the calendar if you can so members can book direct from the site.

Day Twenty-Five: Action Steps

1. **Set up the community option** that you decided on in day 8.

2. **Add any introductory content** that you might need. This could be 'sticky' forum posts with additional information, or group rules in a Facebook group.

3. **Have some conversation starters ready!** Make a spreadsheet of questions and topics that you can use to create discussion.

Website Essentials

Today is a very practical day looking at some additional tools that you might want to consider using for your site. Some of these are essentials and others are entirely dependent on your needs and wants.

Most (but not all) of the tools we're going to talk about here are WordPress plugins. If you're using a different system it's worth looking into what's available with similar functionality.

A note about plugins: plugins are great for adding functionality, there's no doubt about it. When it comes to plugins though, more isn't better. In fact, the aim with your site should be to achieve the functionality you want with the minimum of plugins.

Why? Because each plugin you add to your site increases the chance of conflicts and compatibility issues (in other words, plugins not playing nicely with each other and causing errors!).

Also, depending on the plugins, a large plugin load can lead to performance issues such as slow loading, which you definitely don't want.

You're also more likely to do the 'please no white screen of death' prayer every time you need to update WordPress and any of your other plugins!

So, think about whether you really need to use a plugin for what you want to achieve. And be sure to do a bit of research before you install anything to make sure there aren't any known issues or that the plugin is still be maintained and supported. Checking the plugin homepage is a good place to start

The essential tools:

- **Security** – keep your site as secure as possible from hackers and malicious scripts with a security plugin. Popular choices are *Sucuri scanner, Wordfence* and *iThemes Security*.
- **Limit logins** – as another security measure put something in place to limit the number of login attempts someone can make (your membership plugin may have this feature already though, so check first). *Login Lockdown* is a good choice here or *Limit Logins* (no longer updated but still works well).
- **Backup** – backing up any WP site is important. With a membership site it's absolutely vital (when you've got paying members you want to make sure you can quickly get your site back up and running!) There are a wide range of options here but some of the best known are *VaultPress, BackupBuddy* or *Updraft Plus*.
- **Analytics** – it's a good idea to keep track of visits to your site and pages being seen and we also find it useful to setup goals to track things like sales. *Google Analytics* is the obvious choice here and we tend to install the code manually, but if you'd prefer a plugin to do this for you then take a look at *Google Analytics by Yoast* and *Google Analyticator*.

Some optional tools:

- **Tracking pixels** – If you're going to be running Facebook ads, Google Adwords (or anything else requiring tracking pixels or special code) then you want an easy way to put these on the relevant pages. We recommend a plugin called *Header and Footer Scripts*, which will allow you to add the relevant code without having to edit your theme files.

- **Search Engine Optimisation** – I'd consider this essential for a normal website, but for a membership site you generally don't want your site to appear in search. However, if your membership is attached to a front facing website or blog or you're using a Paywall you'll definitely want this. Our preference is *Yoast SEO*, but *All-In-One SEO* is also a popular option.
- **Caching** – caching essentially helps to improve the speed of your site. However, it's not generally recommended for logged in members for a variety of reasons, and can cause issues with some membership plugins. If you'd like to try it for your front-end pages try *W3 Total Cache* or *WP Super Cache*.
- **Image optimisation** – the best way to optimize your images is by doing it before you upload them to your site (i.e., upload the size you need, not a 2000px image for a 200px space). If it's too late for that though, try *EWWW Image Optimizer* or *WP Smush*, which will reduce your image file size without affecting the quality.
- **Affiliate links** – if you're going to be using affiliate links you can use a plugin to provide an easier (and better looking) link to share. Take a look at *Pretty Link Lite* or *Thirsty Affiliates*, which will enable you to "mask" the affiliate link with something a bit neater
- **Spam** – for a paid members only site you shouldn't need to worry about spam. However if you're running a blog with comments or a free membership level you might want to install the *Akismet* plugin or look at adding a recaptcha or honey-pot to your sign-ups.
- **Helpdesk** – if you want a central system to deal with support requests take a look at the *WATS* plugin, or non plugin software

like *Help Scout, Intercom* and *Zendesk*, which will enable members to submit support tickets that are easier for you to manage than having them send emails.

- **Forms** – if you want to have different forms like contact, support, questions etc then look at a plugin like *Contact Form 7, Ninja Forms, Fast Secure Contact Form* or (our favourite) *Gravity Forms.*

- **Live Chat** - giving potential members a way of interacting with you and asking questions via your sales page can often boost signups. Popular services such as *LiveChatInc* have their own plugins to connect with WordPress

Day Twenty-Six: Action Steps

1. **Make sure you've got your essentials covered** – especially security and backups.

2. Consider what **non-essential plugins** you would like to use and get these installed and set up

Creating Your Sales Page

By now you should have an idea of everything you need to build your site. However there's one important thing left – your sales page.

You know now exactly what you're going to be offering to people, how much you're going to charge for it and whether you're going to offer any launch pricing or bonuses, so it's the perfect time to create your sales page.

Now, any Google search will bring up countless guides and strategies for writing a sales page that sells, and some things come down to personal taste and the type of product that you're offering.

However, we find it's great to start with a simple 8 part process (that should work for any product!) and flesh things out from there as needed.

Our 8 step sales page process:

1. **Create a compelling headline and sub headlines** – your headline needs to give an immediate idea of your membership sites value so that they want to read more. Your sub-headlines are important for drawing in skim readers.
2. **Address the core problem** – what is the main issue your audience has? Use your copy to tap into the feelings it brings up for them – or try telling a story about where they are now and where they will be after they join your membership.
3. **Talk about your solution** – how are you going to solve their problem? How will they feel after joining your membership? How do they know this membership is right for them? Focus on the benefits and the results, not the features.
4. **Provide social proof** – include testimonials, social media

mentions or 'as featured in' accreditations. If you don't yet have any testimonials for this membership then do you have testimonials about you and your services that would be relevant in showing your expertise in this area?

5. **Introduce yourself** – who are you and why should they trust you? What makes your understand this issue and why have you created this membership? (if you're unknown by most of your audience, move this higher up the page).

6. **Discuss the features and details** – what exactly are they getting if they join? Break it down into specifics so they know what to expect.

7. **Present your offer** – be clear about your pricing and tell them exactly what to do if they want to buy. Create a custom call to action rather than just 'Join' (make sure your CTA - Call to Action - visually stands out too). Mention any time limits, deadlines, bonuses or guarantees.

8. **Answer FAQs** – what questions might people have? What might not be clear? Answer these in advance and put their mind at ease!

Hopefully this gives you a good starting point for writing your sales page copy.

Some notes on design

You may decide that some of this information is best covered in a video rather than as text (or as well as text), in which case we recommend having the video near the top of your sales page (under your headline) and then using the rest of the page to expand and clarify.

In terms of actually building your sales page then you may be able to create it directly in the theme that you're using, or you may prefer to use a page builder (like OptimizePress or Thrive Content Builder) to give you more control over layout, such as creating rows with different backgrounds to help break up your text (you might want to look back at day 4 and the tutorial on using Thrive if you'd like to use this option).

Whichever option you choose be sure that the style is in keeping with your membership design – use your brand colours and fonts rather than going for a completely different look.

Be sure to make your call to action (the "buy" button!) stand out with a contrasting colour and make use of white space and padding to ensure that your content doesn't look cramped on the page.

Where possible, use images and graphics alongside your text to add variation and visual cues.

Connecting with your membership plugin for payments

Most membership plugins will create your payment link for you once integrated with your payment processor, so make sure you know where to find this in your plugin settings and remember to add it to every CTA button on your sales page.

If you're offering different prices (i.e. annual and monthly or basic and VIP) then make sure the different pricing is clear and check that you are using the right payment links for each (you'd be surprised how easy it is to use the wrong link!).

Remember, if you're taking payments on your site rather than redirecting to PayPal, your payment link should begin with https:// not http:// in order to ensure that the payment process is secure. In fact your payment processor will almost certainly have this as a requirement of taking on-site card payments.

You'll need to purchase and install an SSL certificate in order to add this level of security; while there are multiples places to buy SSL certificates the simplest option is to simply ask your hosting company to provide this for you.

There will be a cost associated but this is typically no more than $100 per year.

Day Twenty-Seven: Action Steps

1. **Go through our 8 step process** and write a first draft of your sales page content.

2. **Put your draft to one side** and think about how you could layout your content on your sales page (we find sketching it out works well!).

3. **Start to create your sales page** on your website.

4. Tomorrow, **come back to your sales page draft** and see any areas that need trimming or expanding (editing is always easier the next day!).

Really not sure of the kind of design you want for your site? Take a look at other people's sales pages and see what you like and what appeals to you.

Setting Your Members Up for Success

We're on the home straight now and hopefully your membership site is beginning to take shape and become a reality. Today we're going to be looking at an important, but often overlooked, part of the membership process: member onboarding.

What is member onboarding?

Put simply, it's the process that you put in place to help your members acquire the knowledge and skills that they need to use your membership site.

It's all about helping members to start off on the right foot, so that they get the best from their membership (and are less likely to want to leave!).

Ideally your onboarding will:

- Remove any technical challenges
- Deliver immediate value
- Integrate the member into your community
- Encourage content consumption
- Reward desired behaviours

The result of a good onboarding process is more engaged members who achieve better results. Which is a win all round!

What not to do

- Don't just send the default sign-up email that comes with your membership plugin! Usually this will be something along the lines of 'Hi, here's your login details'. Not the most welcoming first message for your newly paid up member!

- Don't assume that it's obvious where they need to start or what they should do first – lay out the next steps for them.

Some onboarding methods you could use:

- **Welcome email** – make your first email count. Make them feel welcome and valued, let them know what to expect and how to get started.
- **Getting started guide** – give them all the information and steps they need to get going with your site and find anything they might need.
- **Walkthrough video** – create a video showing them around your site and all the different areas they have access to.
- **Email sequence** – set up a sequence of emails that will gradually introduce them to your site and all its different features.
- **On-site messaging** – use a system like Intercom.io to deliver onboarding messages when the member logs on to your site.
- **Orientation webinar** – you may want to hold a webinar (how often depends on your site) for new members that walks them through things live and answers any questions they have directly.
- **Content paths** – if you have a lot of content, consider creating suggested 'content paths' to help people know where to start based on their goals.

You may want to combine a couple of methods – such as a welcome email and a walkthrough video – and we'd generally recommend that most sites would benefit from incorporating an email sequence aimed at new members.

The methods that work for you, and how in-depth your onboarding needs to be, depends entirely on the kind of membership you're creating.

If it's a simple course then a welcome email may be enough, but if it's an ongoing membership site with lots of different content types and a forum then you're going to want a longer and more involved process.

If you're running a trial or offering a guarantee, consider having your onboarding process cover this time period, including regular check-ins.

In reality there's no hard and fast rules when it comes to member onboarding and you may want to test some different options to see what gives you the best results.

The most important thing is that you don't leave your new members floundering.

Day Twenty-Eight: Action Steps

1. Before anything else, **customize the default welcome email** that comes with your membership plugin!

2. Take a look at your membership site and **make a note of anything you think a new member might need to know.**

3. **Decide on the best way for you to communicate those things** – is it a walkthrough video, a series of emails or something else?

Putting Your Site Through its Paces

Once your site is all set up and ready to go, there's just one last thing to do. Test, test and test some more!

It's important to test every aspect of your site – you want to make sure that you test your whole member journey.

Both so that you know that everything works and also so that you're 100% sure of what the process for your customers actually is.

This includes testing payments too so make sure you test your checkout process!

The main things you need to test:

- **User friendliness** – is the site easy for your members to use and navigate? Is it obvious what everything is and how things work?
- **Functionality** – does everything work the way that it should? Make sure to test things like user profiles as well.
- **Responsiveness** – does the site work well on tablets and mobiles? Remember to check everything – from your checkout process to your member content.
- **Site speed** – does your site load quickly? Slow loading sites can cause you to lose both visitors and members.
- **Different browsers** – test your site in different browsers to make sure that it works in each. Be aware that it might not look identical across the board though.

If there are any leaks, weaknesses or areas of uncertainty then see how you can remedy this and, if needed, be sure to cover any areas of difficulty or ambiguity in your member onboarding (e.g. if your forum is a little more tricky to use than you thought, accommodate this by creating a walkthrough video for your members, or if your videos can't be viewed on iPhones, let members know this in advance).

Ideally though you want to correct any issues as much as possible before you start letting your members onboard.

Consider running a beta test

It's definitely advisable for you to test your whole site thoroughly before you let your first members in the door.

But, it can also be useful to get some other people to test the site for you too – they may notice things that you haven't, and can give you some valuable feedback on your functionality and user friendliness.

There are two main types of beta test. One is a small free beta test by friends, colleagues or trusted audience members. The other is more of a 'mini launch' where you run a paid (albeit at a lower cost than you will charge at your main launch) beta test for the people on your waitlist.

Whichever you choose, in order to get the most from the beta test you may want to provide your testers with specific questions or a checklist or survey for them to complete to ensure thorough feedback.

Running a small beta test is definitely a great way of thoroughly putting your site through its paces, and an added bonus is that you can also ask your beta testers to provide a testimonial for your sales page.

Questions to ask yourself when creating your beta test...

Will your beta test be free or paid?

You may initially think that a beta test should be free. However it can actually work out better for both you and your beta members to have a fee attached.

It's typical that people will often place less value on free, whereas if there is a payment involved it provides added incentive to actually make use of and engage with the content.

So typically we recommend a paid beta unless you're inviting a select number of existing peers to try out the site for you.

The beta price should be heavily discounted however, not your normal membership price. It could even be that you give a low cost lifetime option.

How long will your beta last?

Your beta test can be as long or as short as you want and to a certain extent this will depend on the type of content that you're providing. Typically 2 -4 weeks works well for most though.

If your members have access to everything straight away then you may want to keep the test short and run it for just a couple of weeks.

On the other hand if your content is being drip fed then you will probably want to give it a bit longer in order for members to experience the content dripping.

Basically you want to ensure that your test is long enough for your members to experience as much of the site as possible, but short enough to keep up momentum and interest.

Where will you get your beta members from?

There are a number of ways to attract your beta members and the best approach for you may depend on factors such as your existing audience and whether it's a free or paid test.

If you already have a group of trusted people in your target audience then these can be ideal to use for your beta testers. This approach can work well when you already want to give a few free accounts to your peers or specific community members.

You may also invite a select number of people from your existing community, or wait list, who are highly engaged with your content. This approach can work for either a free or paid test.

Or you could send out an open invite, allowing anyone who wants to to sign up, until a certain number of members has been reached. This approach should only really be used for a paid test.

Whichever option you choose, remember that you want to ensure that your beta members are your target audience. Otherwise their feedback on things like your content may not be as valuable.

What kind of feedback will you ask for?

To get the most from your beta test you need to get quality feedback from your beta members on all aspects of their site experience.

What did they like about the site? Was there anything that didn't make sense? Did the site function well? What would have made their experience better?

You get the picture!

Decide in advance the questions that you will ask your beta testers. It may even be that you ask them different questions at different stages of the test, for example some initial questions after their first few days and then more in-depth questions near the end.

Also consider how you will collect the feedback. You could simply rely on your community for this but a survey works best in our experience for gathering specific information.

I also recommend making it a condition of their continued membership that they complete any feedback requests.

Day Twenty-Nine: Action Steps

1. **Test your site!** Go through your site with a fine tooth comb, check it in various browsers and on mobile and tablet. Then test out your complete customer journey, from your sales page to accessing your content.

2. **Consider running a beta test** to get other peoples feedback on your site too.

DAY 30

Launching Your Membership

Woo hoo! You made it to the end!

Even if you haven't implemented everything as you went along hopefully you now have a good idea of the steps you can take to go from idea to launch with your membership site, when the time is right.

That last thing for us to discuss is your launch itself. It's always a nerve racking time putting your hard work out into the world so if you're feeling a bit anxious or unsure, that's all par for the course.

Once your first member signs up then you'll remember what you've been working so hard for!

Before you open the doors to your site though, there's a few pre-launch checks that you can do to make sure everything runs smoothly.

Pre-launch checklist:

- ☐ **Let your payment processor know that you're launching** so that they don't put your account on hold if there's a spike in payments or anything that they might consider 'unusual activity' for your account.
- ☐ **Let your hosting provider know too** so that they can provide additional resources for your site if there is a spike in traffic (the last thing you want is for your site to go down!).
- ☐ **Use an uptime monitor** (like uptimerobot.com which is free) to keep an eye on things and ensure you catch any issues early. These services will email you if your site goes down, so you're not caught unaware.
- ☐ **Take a backup of everything** before you open the doors!

- ☐ **Have support in place** for your members in case they have any issues – and know who you can get in touch with too if something goes wrong.
- ☐ **Let your advocates know** that you're launching and would appreciate their support with your marketing efforts.

Launch Day

Once you've run through the pre-launch checklist and got all your ducks in a row, it's time to take a deep breath and open your membership site.

You may decide to launch to your waitlist first and then launch to the general public a few days later, or you may launch to everyone straight away.

Either way you should email your waitlist first with the news and if you aren't giving them early access to the site then you may want to consider giving them a special discount or bonus instead.

You've tested your site beforehand so there shouldn't be any nasty surprises on launch day, but if there are any teething issues when your members start joining then try and take it in your stride rather than getting stressed – these things happen and aren't usually the end of the world (need emergency support for tech stuff? Try a service like WPCurve.com).

You should already have a plan for your launch marketing, but make sure that you stagger your promotional activity so that people aren't bombarded and liable to launch fatigue.

It's also good to remember that for an ongoing membership site you're looking at more of a long game with your marketing, so you don't necessarily need to go all out trying to get everyone through the door at once.

What if your launch isn't a success?

Nobody wants to think about their launch not doing well, but it can and does happen.

Remember though that just because you didn't hit your launch targets it doesn't make it a failure.

And, if you're running an evergreen membership site particularly, your success isn't dependent just on your launch, so whilst things may be a slower burn than you hoped, don't be disheartened.

Day Thirty: Action Steps

1. **Run the pre-launch checklist** and make sure you've got everything covered.

2. **Finalise your launch marketing plan** (look back at the day 3 worksheet!)

3. **Take a deep breath and launch!**

What Now?

Congratulations on launching your membership website!

Most people don't realise just how much is involved in planning, building and launching a membership, so you should be proud to get this far.

However, your work is not done.

Memberships are a marathon, not a sprint - so the real work has just begun.

Some time within the next few weeks your initial launch period is going to end, the buzz, hype and excitement surrounding your grand opening will subside and it will be over to you to settle into your role as a membership site owner.

You'll find that you have plenty to occupy you day to day just with dealing with members and creating content; but it's important not to let the momentum of your launch slip away.

Now is the time to get into "Maintenance Marketing Mode" for your membership - growing and nurturing your email list, continuing to reinforce your credibility as an expert through strategies like content marketing, experimenting with different tactics for driving member sales.

Whatever you do, however, don't fall into the trap of thinking that simply attracting new members is all that matters.

With a membership site it's as important, if not more so, that you hang onto the members you bring in; otherwise you miss out on one of the best things about memberships - recurring revenue. If you're not retaining, that revenue won't be recurring.

With most other types of "transactional" business, the sale is the end result. With memberships, it's just the beginning. It's down to you to show up and serve your audience.

To keep people paying you on a recurring basis, you need to deliver value on a recurring basis too.

Continue looking for the best way to serve your audience; strive for find better solutions for their problems, challenges and obstacles. Keep trying to innovate and improve your membership, using the feedback in input you get from members to guide and shape the direction you take your website in.

Overall have fun with it. You need to enjoy what you're doing otherwise it will show in the effort you put into creating content, providing solutions and interacting with your community.

The great thing is that nothing in your membership is set in stone.

No longer enjoy creating courses? Create something else! Members not as interested as you thought they'd be in that fancy widget you built them? Scrap it! The best memberships are always a work in progress; continuously evolving, testing and adapting.

It won't be a cake-walk. Figuring out the best way to keep your membership growing, how to attract members and keep the ones you have is challenging.

It's easy to see why a lot of membership sites fail, or simply never get off the ground. It's because there's nowhere to turn to get the support and knowledge needed to get it done right!

That's the reason that we created the Member Site Academy to provide you with all the training, support, accountability, knowledge and feedback that will make you membership site a success…

When you're a part of the Member Site Academy, you get access to:

- Our unique Membership Roadmap that takes you step by step through everything you need to do whether you're planning, creating, launching or growing your membership.
- An extensive library of courses & training materials covering all aspects of planning, building and growing your membership website.
- Monthly live training calls and mastermind sessions to deep dive into topics as well as answer all your questions.
- A resources section with discounts, tools and exclusive plugins only for Academy members.
- Community forums, where you can discuss any challenges you're having, get technical assistance, discuss strategy and receive advice, support and encouragement from ourselves and other members.

If you're serious about building a successful membership website, then the Member Site Academy is a no-brainer; and to make it even easier for you to get the knowledge and resources you need, we're offering a **FREE 14 Day Trial** for readers of Member Machine to enable you to take it for a test drive.

And in the very unlikely chance that you don't find it useful you can cancel in 2 clicks without ever needing to contact us.

Tools and Resources

We're frequently asked for our favourite tools and resources for building membership sites.

You'll find our recommendations below.

Membership Plugins

MemberPress – the plugin we use for our own membership, the Member Site Academy. *www.themembershipguys.com/mp*

s2Member Pro – a long-standing plugin with a great free option. *www.themembershipguys.com/s2m*

Paid Memberships Pro – a sturdy free plugin extendable through extensive add-ons. Also comes with a free membership-centric WordPress theme. *www.paidmembershipspro.com*

Wishlist Member – more payment integrations than any other option. *www.themembershipguys.com/wishlist*

MemberMouse – MemberMouse has some features, like one-click upsells, not available in other options. *www.themembershipguys.com/membermouse*

Memberium – great option for Infusionsoft or ActiveCampaign based memberships (the ActiveCampaign version is free) *www.memberium.com*

AccessAlly – stylish option for Infusionsoft, Ontraport or ActiveCampaign based memberships. *www.themembershipguys.com/msaaccessally*

ActiveMember360 – another great option for anyone using ActiveCampaign, allowing for a powerful tag-based membership
www.activemember360.com

Woo Memberships – selling multiple different products is easy with WooCommerce and Woo Memberships.
www.woocommerce.com/products/woocommerce-memberships

iThemes Exchange – another ecommerce based option.
www.themembershipguys.com/ithemesx

Restrict Content Pro – a lightweight option that is great for simple sites, those needing group memberships or for developers to extend.
www.restrictcontentpro.com

Course Plugins

LifterLMS – an easy to set up free LMS plugin with inbuilt membership function and stylish course pages.
www.themembershipguys.com/lifterlms

WPCourseware – a lightweight LMS that can be added to any site and integrates with most membership plugin.
www.themembershipguys.com/wpcourse

LearnDash – the LMS heavyweight, which includes a wealth of powerful features for running multiple online courses.
www.themembershipguys.com/learndash

WPEP – a unique accordion style layout to courses to keep things simple and streamlined. *www.themembershipguys.com/wpep*

Themes & Page Builders

Divi – very flexible theme with inbuilt page builder that can be used for most kinds of sites. *www.themembershipguys.com/elegantthemes*

Thrive Themes – marketing focused themes and an excellent content builder plugin for creating landing pages. *www.themembershipguys.com/thrive*

Boss Theme – purely focused on BuddyPress and ideal for a community based site. *www.themembershipguys.com/bosstheme*

Beaver Builder – can be used for creating your entire site or just for landing pages. *www.themembershipguys.com/beaverbuilder*

OptimizePress – landing pages, a theme, membership plugin. You can create your whole membership with OP. *www.themembershipguys.com/op2*

Community Software

IP.Board – an excellent forum software that we personally use for the Academy community. *www.invisionpower.com*

bbPress - popular free forum plugin for WordPress created by the guys who built WordPress itself. *www.bbpress.org*

BuddyPress - widely used free plugin which turns WordPress into a complete social network. *www.buddypress.org*

Discourse - modern and stylish community discussion software. Cloud-based, but can be linked to WordPress. *www.discourse.org*

Other Tools

AffiliateWP – our favourite affiliate plugin which offers a great core plugin and add-ons for additional features.
www.themembershipguys.com/affiliatewp

LiveChat – an great addition to your sales page, particularly during a launch. *www.themembershipguys.com/livechat*

Intercom – on-site app messaging, great for membership sites and onboarding. *www.intercom.io*

ProgressAlly – add some gamification and progress tracking features to any membership. *www.themembershipguys.com/progressally*

Gravity Forms – far more than just forms! Can also be used for quizzes, payments, conditional content and more.
www.themembershipguys.com/gravityforms

Social Learner – a theme and plugin set specifically for combining LearnDash or Sensei with BuddyPress.
www.themembershipguys.com/sociallearner-learndash

BackupBuddy – it's vital to keep your membership site backed up!
www.ithemes.com/backupbuddy

WooCommerce – a great ecommerce store for selling all kind of products – physical, digital or membership.
www.woocommerce.com

Easy Digital Downloads – excellent for adding a lightweight store selling digital downloads. *www.easydigitaldownloads.com*

Clickfunnels – cloud platform which can be used for creating your whole sales funnel, with sales pages, landing pages and even basic content protection. *www.themembershipguys.com/clickfunnels*

Email Marketing

ActiveCampaign – powerful automations, tagging and our personal choice for email marketing. *www.themembershipguys.com/activecampaign*

Mailchimp – a good starter option (but not great if you want multiple lead magnets and advanced automation.) *www.mailchimp.com*

Convertkit – a good middle ground between Mailchimp and ActiveCampaign. *www.themembershipguys.com/convertkit*

Other Books we Recommend

The Membership Economy by Robbie Kellman Baxter

The Automatic Customer by John Warrillow

Buzzing Communities by Richard Millington

Subscription Marketing by Anne H Janzer

Hooked by Nir Eyal

Will It Fly by Pat Flynn

Evergreen by Noah Fleming

Available on Amazon and in all good bookstores!

From The Membership Guys

The Membership Guys Blog – regular articles and resources to help make your membership a success. *www.themembershipguys.com*

The Membership Guys Podcast – weekly dose of proven, practical tips to grow your membership. *www.membershippodcast.com*

Membership Mastermind – our free Facebook group for membership site owners. *www.talkmemberships.com*

Member Site Academy – all of the step-by-step training, support and exclusive resources you need to plan, build, launch and grow your membership website. *www.membersiteacademy.com*

Connect With Us

We'd love to connect with you and hear about your membership site, what you thought of this book and anything else you've got going on. Hook up with us on one of the below platforms and say "Hi!"...

Twitter – @membershipguys

Facebook – facebook.com/membershipguys

YouTube – youtube.com/themembershipguys

Instagram – instagram.com/membershipguy

Disclaimer: *Some of the resources contained in this book and in the list above may include affiliate codes that result in us receiving a small commission on any purchases. This doesn't increase the price you pay and does not influence our recommendations. We only include links to products that we genuinely believe in and have used or researched.*

Printed in Great Britain
by Amazon